Government publishing in the Canadian provinces

Government publishing in the Canadian provinces

A PRESCRIPTIVE STUDY

A. PAUL PROSS and CATHERINE A. PROSS

University of Toronto Press

© University of Toronto Press 1972

Toronto and Buffalo

Printed in Canada

Reprinted in 2018

ISBN 0-8020-1827-0

Microfiche ISBN 0-8020-0150-5

ISBN 978-1-4875-8156-5 (paper)

LC 77-166936

For
Canada's Provincial Legislative Librarians
past and present

They and their colleagues have worked with
monumental devotion to ensure that at least one library
in each province houses a comprehensive collection
of provincial publications. But for them, much
of this heritage must have disappeared completely.

Foreword

This study will interest every citizen concerned with the fabric of political life and democratic government in Canada. No one who reads it with a minimum of attention can any longer remain indifferent towards the whole problem of the inadequacy of provincial government publication in Canada.

This study approaches the problem of provincial government publication with a commendable democratic and scholarly perspective. It rightly underlines such important problems as that of defining provincial government publications and provides conceptual remedies, long overdue, for obvious deficiencies in existing governmental structures for the processing and the distribution of such publications throughout Canada. It is not, however, only a "prescriptive study," as its title says, but a very perceptive description of government publishing in the Canadian provinces; it is thorough in scope and incisive in its conclusions and recommendations.

It may be significant that this study was undertaken contemporaneously with what its authors call "the apparent resurgence of provincial power within the Canadian federal system" and that the authors' first requests for information and assistance met with reasonably good response from all provinces but Quebec. It does reflect in a very real sense the difficulties now facing the country and particularly the cultural cleavages now putting Confederation under some considerable strain.

The Canadian Political Science Association is grateful to Paul and Catherine Pross for this study. It is particularly proud of its sponsorship of their report, for it senses that the report will contribute greatly to bringing attention in Canada to bear on an important and pressing matter. Naturally, the Association will consider with utmost care the conclusions and recommendations of the study, and do what it can to check the present disastrous decentralization of provincial government publications in Canada. In so doing, the Canadian Political Science Association will be carrying out one of its primary tasks - to facilitate research and to promote in every possible way the advancement of political studies in Canada - and it hopes that this report may have an even wider importance in improving the responsible functioning of our government.

Gilles Lalande
President (1970-1)
Canadian Political Science Association

Acknowledgments

This report is a compilation of data painstakingly accumulated by scholars, administrators, and librarians across the country. We have no accurate count of their number, but they are many. They assisted us with great good humour and patience because they believed that the purpose of the project was worthwhile. In thanking them, we hope that they will feel that their time and energy have not been abused.

The Canadian Political Science Association sponsored the project and, with the Institute of Public Administration of Canada, has aided in its publication. To thank these institutions is to thank the men who acted as their and our advisers: Peter Russell, T.H. Qualter, Robert Fenn, W.E. Grasham, David Hoffman, Peter Silcox, Fred Schindeler, Douglas Verney, Michael Goldrick, and David E. Smith.

No less important was the assistance of the Canada Council, which generously supported our research and sympathetically heard our inevitable requests for deadline extensions. Both were greatly appreciated.

As the report neared completion we asked a small, knowledgeable group to read and comment upon the final draft. Miss Jean Kerfoot, Legislative Librarian of Ontario, Miss Shirley Elliott, Legislative Librarian of Nova Scotia, Mr S.W. Smith of the Advisory Services Division, Ontario Treasury Board Secretariat, Mr D. Tudor, Librarian, Ontario Department of Revenue, and Dr Olga Bishop, School of Library Science, University of Toronto, suggested additions, pointed out omissions, and corrected errors.

Douglas Verney, of the Department of Political Science, York University, and Alan MacDonald, Assistant Librarian, Dalhousie University, must receive special mention. Douglas Verney, reviewing the manuscript at that critical moment when most authors tire of polishing and ache to see their efforts rendered into type, not only goaded us into performing some valuable plastic surgery, but provided the encouragement needed to make the task seem worthwhile. Alan MacDonald enthusiastically gave advice and assistance throughout the research and writing phases of the study. On several occasions he was an invaluable liaison with the library community. Much of the study could not have been written without his help.

Our friends have attempted to save us from folly and we are grateful for all that they have done. But, with the best will in the world, they cannot stop every leak nor mend every sail, so as we launch this frail craft we hasten to assure them that if we sink there must be no one to blame but ourselves.

Finally we wish to thank Mrs Heather Holdway, Earl Whynot, of Earl Whynot & Associates Limited, and R.I.K. Davidson, of University of Toronto Press, for their assistance in typing and publishing the manuscript.

A. Paul Pross
Catherine A. Pross
Indian Path, N.S.

Contents

Foreword	vii
Acknowledgments	ix
List of tables and charts	xiii
1 The problem	3
2 Problems of definition: the hidden revolution in information technology	12
3 The current model for production	20
4 Publication distribution: government systems	34
Distribution Structures 34	
(i) Atlantic provinces 34	
(ii) Western provinces 38	
(iii) Quebec 41	
(iv) Ontario 41	
Mailing lists 44	
Perpetuation of decentralized systems 46	
5 Output to input: the difficult task of acquiring provincial government publications of	50
Depository libraries 51	
Conclusions 59	
6 Finding aids: uncertain guides to publication production	62
Document discovery 62	
Canadiana 65	
Bibliographies and checklists of provincial publications 68	
7 Existing library resources	83
Strength of collections 83	

Hansard 116
Royal Commission materials 117
Election data 118
Publications on microfilm 119
Access 120
General comments and conclusions 121

8 Organization of collections 123
    Separate vs. integrated collections 123
    Cataloguing and classification systems 126
    Automation 129

9 The underdeveloped role of provincial legislative libraries 132

10 Recommendations 140

    Summary of recommendations 156

    Appendix I: The questionnaire 161

    Appendix II: legislative authorization of depository status 177

Tables and charts

TABLE	1:1	Distribution of questionnaires and responses by province	8
TABLE	1:2	Responses to questionnaire 5 (users) showing geographic location of academics engaged in research in provincial studies and incidence of teaching activity in the field	9
TABLE	3:1	Statutory provision for publication by Queen's Printer	22
TABLE	3:2	Duties of the Queen's Printers: data from questionnaires 1 (Queen's Printers) and 2 (government departments)	23
CHART	3:1	The stages of production	24
TABLE	4:1	Distributors of selected categories of Atlantic provinces publications	37
TABLE	4:2	Distributors of selected categories of western provinces publications	39
TABLE	4:3	Distributors of selected categories of Ontario and Quebec publications	40
TABLE	5:1	Provincial libraries reporting and/or accorded depository status for provincial government publications	52
TABLE	6:1	Sources of provincial publications listed in *Canadiana*	67
TABLE	7:1	Holdings of Newfoundland publications	86
TABLE	7:2	Holdings of Prince Edward Island publications	90
TABLE	7:3	Holdings of Nova Scotia publications	92

TABLE 7:4	Holdings of New Brunswick publications	96
TABLE 7:5	Holdings of Quebec publications	98
TABLE 7:6	Holdings of Ontario publications	102
TABLE 7:7	Holdings of Manitoba publications	104
TABLE 7:8	Holdings of Saskatchewan publications	108
TABLE 7:9	Holdings of Alberta publications	110
TABLE 7:10	Holdings of British Columbia publications	114
CHART 10:1	A suggested operating structure for an official publisher and printer	146
CHART 10:2	Publication production and distribution flow in a centralized service	148

Government publishing in the Canadian provinces

1
The problem

Extreme decentralization of provincial government publishing systems has rendered it extremely difficult, almost impossible, to locate, obtain, and eventually utilize the information generated by and for provincial public authorities. These difficulties apply whether the would-be user is an interested citizen, a public official, or an academic. They threaten, not simply the scholarly study of provincial affairs, but also the fabric of political life at the middle level of Canadian government.

At first glance a picture of rampant confusion, the current state of affairs can be analysed in terms of five central problems, which must be resolved in the course of making democratic government meaningful, the policy process efficient, and academic study reflect the mass of data that can be made available.

At the outset there is a problem of definition: there is no clear description of what a provincial government publication actually is, a deficiency that perplexes government officials and frustrates members of the public as they haggle over the status of particular documents.

Second, and at the heart of the current unsatisfactory situation, is the excessive diffusion of government structures for processing and distributing publications. The agencies involved in publishing provincial documents are so many and so varied that they often defy identification by interested outsiders.

Decentralization in turn compounds the difficulties created by two further impediments to governmental communication with the governed. There is no adequate procedure for the "discovery" of documents and there are no effective depository systems operating at the provincial level in Canada. The first means that there is no method of ensuring that the existence of a document will ever be established by librarians, and hence there is no way to guarantee its inclusion in bibliographies and other finding aids. Without depository systems - structures that ensure that the majority of government publications are sent to designated libraries - Canadians cannot even be sure that the most basic of provincial government documents will be available locally; at present the only documents normally sent to major libraries as a matter of course are statutes; others are on the shelves as the result of the diligence and patience of acquisitions librarians. A common situation is cited by a New Brunswick economist: "I have mainly used the annual reports of the Departments of Labor. To my knowledge, there is no complete collection of these east of McGill. On occasion I have had to borrow the sole copy possessed by the department itself for some year in the recent past."[1]

Finally, there are no adequate library procedures for handling provincial publications. Arrangements for reporting and locating them are few and unreliable and there are no automated systems devised that are capable of retrieving the information contained in this vast data bank.

Expressed more briefly, the tangle of difficulties impeding the effective use of provincial publications can be ordered into the five general problem areas of definition, diffusion, discovery, deposit, and library procedures.

The reality behind this sparse catalogue is the subject of the following study, but it can be illustrated here. In particular, excessive decentralization is exemplified by the fact that each of Canada's ten provincial governments embraces about twenty separate agencies, every one of which may publish and distribute between one and a dozen publications annually.[2] Their production processes vary enormously. There are well-equipped, knowledgeable teams of experts and editors who would fit easily into the structure of a major publishing house. There are others who fall very far indeed below this level. The equipment used by one agency may be efficient, modern, and appropriate to its publishing responsibilities; that of another may be totally inadequate, while a third organization may boast excessive overcapacity. In all likelihood there will exist no means of co-ordinating the use of these resources.

The product, too, is variable. Some provincial publications are lavish productions, overflowing with colour photographs and elaborate charts. Others are modest in the extreme. Style of presentation, however, is seldom a guide to the utility of a document. The 1968 report of the Ontario Council for the Arts - a "bright, beautiful" succession of photographs interspersed with short declarations such as "we throw pebbles" - was justly dismissed by Ontario M.L.A. Elmer Sopha as "psychedelic flapdoodle", while the equally attractive Hall-Dennis report, *Living and Learning,* has become perhaps the most widely read study of education ever published in this country.[3] Finally, provincial publishers observe few standards to ensure clear presentation of subject matter, and consistency in reporting is equally rare.

In the distribution of publications the atomism of these systems achieves its apotheosis. The librarian, the researcher, and certainly members of the general public encounter innumerable obstacles whenever they attempt to discover, first, whether desired information is available in published form, and then, if it is, where access may be obtained to the document in question. Normally reliable finding aids are virtually useless in this field, and even narrowly focused bibliographies are notoriously inadequate, for the simple reason that their compilers cannot make good the deficiencies of distribution systems that fail to deposit major documents on library shelves.

Locating the source of certain types of publications partially alleviates these problems, but not always. Each librarian or scholar in this field finds that he achieves little by inscribing his name on the mailing list of every agency whose publications he wishes to receive. He must constantly ensure that his name remains on the lists and must scrutinize closely all agency materials, newspaper reports, and legislative documents in the hope of learning of crucial but undistributed documents. Even with this diligence, a personal relationship with agency officials is often the only means by which the existence of many publications will be discovered and, once discovered, obtained. Few libraries and fewer scholars have the resources this procedure demands.

In fact, one cannot guess the costs the existing structure imposes at the governmental and library levels: the weakness of most major libraries in this field suggests that they are prohibitive.[4] The costs to scholarship and to the exercise of democratic control of government by an informed public are beyond calculation.

Nevertheless, it would be foolish to hold governments entirely responsible for the present unsatisfactory situation. Governmental agencies allot their limited resources in response to and in accordance with the pressures and priorities established by their publics: when the public itself has been slow to recognize a need, it is hardly fair to expect governments to provide an advanced and up-to-date service. Some blame, at least, must be accepted by the academic community, which is particularly well placed to observe the need, but which has been slow to recognize its responsibilities in this regard. In particular, the provinces have been badly served by the social sciences. Preoccupied with nationhood, disdaining regionalism, analysts have served the whole at the expense of the parts. Delighting in the broad brush, we have dabbled in macro-analysis, forgetting that successful generalization depends upon painstaking investigation of the constituent microcosms. The resulting hiatus in regional and provincial studies has not only contributed to the shortcoming in provincial government publishing discussed in this study, it has also left social scientists ill-prepared to proffer competent advice to both government and public on the problems presently confronting Canada's provincial and municipal authorities. An increasingly alert public closely observing provincial administrations has every right to expect to be better served by the scholars and librarians on whom the burden of providing adequate information rests.

Although a respectable literature investigates the political life of Canadians at the national level and several studies have examined the history, the economy, or the politics of individual provinces, only one comparative study of Canada *and* its provinces has ever been undertaken.[5] That study appeared in 1917. No authoritative history of Ontario has ever been published, and those of other provinces need updating.[6] Biographies of provincial public figures are few and too often are the effusions of relatives and friends.[7] Political scientists have published general studies of only three provincial governments: Prince Edward Island, Nova Scotia, and Manitoba.[8] No one has attempted to analyse the entire political system of any one province, although provincial parties have aroused more interest.[9] The learned journals have provided a forum for some discussion of provincial and regional issues, but even their performance has varied considerably. At the national level, the *Canadian Historical Review,* from time to time, and *Canadian Public Administration,* frequently, publish relevant articles. The *Canadian Journal of Economics and Political Science* did virtually nothing to promote this branch of scholarship. It is too soon to assess its successors, the *Canadian Journal of Economics* and the *Canadian Journal of Political Science,* both of which were established in 1967. Provincial and regional journals[10] have sustained interest in the field and promoted valuable discussion. However, their local orientations tend to discourage exploration of comparative problems.

The results of neglect can be observed in the lack of informed public opinion on many issues. Within government itself, insufficient preliminary training in the analysis of provincial problems may force officials to provide their ministers with inadequate policy advice.

In recent years a steadily increasing number of scholars have turned their attention to provincial studies. This may be attributable to the fact that the need for better information has become increasingly evident at both policy-making and academic levels, and because the growth of the social sciences has filled in many gaps in our knowledge of the federal political system. Perhaps also, the apparent resurgence of provincial power within the Canadian political system has encouraged investigators to examine more closely the structure and function of this middle level of government. Too, developments in the behavioural approach to political science have prompted a number of comparative studies of electoral behaviour; new analytical techniques, such as those of David Easton[11] and Gabriel Almond,[12] have encouraged an interest in political cultures and political systems at the provincial level. Elsewhere, the study of provincial public administration has received some encouragement, and a number of scholars have undertaken research in various aspects of provincial-municipal relations.

However, these initiatives have been severely restricted by the inadequacy of existing resources of provincial government publications. In the "pioneer" context of the research environment of provincial studies, the flow of information they represent is crucially important. Erratic, poorly compiled, and generally untrustworthy though they may be, they constitute a significant source of information concerning the past and frequently the present.[13] In too many instances, when departmental and personal records have vanished or are not yet available, they are the total accessible research resource. But the investigator soon discovers that while the resource exists, it needs to be located and rendered usable.

In 1967, concerned about these impediments to scholarship, the Canadian Political Science Association moved to establish a committee to work with the Canadian Library Association "to produce a comprehensive report and a set of recommendations regarding the availability of Canadian provincial government publications to university scholars."[14] This study was established with the support of the Canada Council, to achieve that aim. It was intended to provide:
1. an informed, up-to-date description of: (a) the range of published documents available in each province, (b) the range of unprinted public documents available in each province (e.g., documents associated with Royal Commissions: reports, evidence, submissions, proceedings), (c) the procedures whereby responsibility for the production and distribution of published documents is divided between the Queen's Printer and individual departments in each province, (d) the facilities existing for the deposition of provincial government documents in legislative libraries, provincial archives, the National Library, and in university libraries within and outside the province in which the documents originate, (e) procedures for listing provincial government documents in *Canadiana* or provincial guides or both, and (f) the published and unpublished bibliographies in the field; and
2. a series of proposals leading to the improvement of the procedures now existing.[15]

Data were gathered through circulating questionnaires, following up with interviews, and reviewing the rather sparse literature in the field.

Five separate questionnaires were distributed, each intended to maximize the information obtainable from particular sources: Queen's Printers, government departments, provincial legislative and archival libraries, university libraries and "users" (who were generally academics). The questionnaires, together with a commentary, will be found in Appendix I; discussion here will be confined to an assessment of the quality of the response and to one or two findings related to the preceding analysis of the state of scholarly interest in the field.

In all, 156 questionnaires were returned out of a total of 315 distributed (see Table 1:1). But the rate of return was highest where it was most essential: all Queen's Printers responded; 17 of 20 questionnaires to legislative libraries and archives libraries were returned; 38 university and public libraries responded out of a possible 60 and this figure included all but one of the country's major collections. Only government departments and "users" failed to provide a satisfactory response, and their poor showing, which is analysed in Appendix I, can be attributed to the fact that it was impossible to identify either group very distinctly in advance, so that a great many questionnaires had to be wasted in a scattered, random approach.

The interview stage of the inquiry was begun in mid-May 1968 and continued

TABLE 1:1
Distribution of questionnaires and responses by provinces

Province	Type of questionnaire[a]									
	Questionnaire 1 (Queen's Printers)		Questionnaire 2 (government departments)		Questionnaire 3 (legislative libraries)		Questionnaire 4 (university libraries)		Questionnaire 5 (users)	
	sent	resp.	sent	resp.	sent	resp.	sent	resp.	sent	resp.
Nfld.	1	1	3	3	2	2	1	1	6	3
NS	1	1	3	3	2	2	4	3	21	9
PEI	1	1	3	1	1	1	2	1	6	1
NB	1	1	3	2	2	1	4	1	14	4
Que.	1	1	4	1	2[b]	1	7	4	26	9
Ont.	1	1	3	3	2	2	19	11	82	27
Man.	1	1	3	1	2	1	3	1	10	3
Sask.	1	1	3	1	2	2	1[c]	1	4	4
Alta.	1	1	3	2	2	2	2	2	10	7
BC	1	1	3	3	1	1	4	4	15	4
Others[d]					2	2	13	9		
Totals	10	10[e]	31	20	20	17	60	38	194	71

Grand totals: 315 sent, 156 returned.

[a] Questionnaires sent to provincial Queen's Printers (type 1); selected provincial government departments (type 2); provincial legislative libraries and archives (type 3); university libraries (type 4); and users (type 5).

[b] An interview was carried out at the National Library of Quebec.

[c] An interview was carried out at the Regina campus of the University of Saskatchewan.

[d] "Other" libraries include: type No. 3 - Library of Parliament, Ottawa, and National Library of Canada, Ottawa; type No. 4 - Gosling Memorial Library, St. John's, Nfld.; Montreal Public Library, Montreal, PQ; Toronto Public Library, Toronto, Ont.; The Library, Glenbow Foundation, Calgary, Alta.; Vancouver Public Library, Vancouver, BC; The Library of Parliament, Ottawa; the National Library of Canada, Ottawa; the Library, Duke University, Durham, NC; the Littauer Library, Harvard University; the New York Public Library; the Library of Congress, Washington, DC.

[e] Where the Queen's Printer did not return a questionnaire the interview provided the opportunity to complete one.

for four months with interviews being held in all provincial capitals and almost all major universities. Meetings took place with respondents to the questionnaires, with individuals who were able to provide valuable information but had not responded to the questionnaire, and with others recommended to us as indispensable sources of knowledge concerning past and present practice. This procedure permitted a flexibility impossible if the questionnaires alone had been used. So, for example, when government departments proved incapable of providing an overview of general publishing conditions within the province, valuable assistance was obtained from officials of treasury departments in four provinces and members of the premier's staff in two. In several instances it was found helpful to approach government agencies, academics, and public libraries not consulted at the initial stage of the inquiry.

The data accumulated, in addition to providing essential information concerning the central problem of the study, also revealed something of the extent and growth of academic interest in provincial studies. Of the 71 respondents to the "users" questionnaire, 64 reported themselves carrying out research in the field. Interviews established that another 21 were similarly engaged. As suggested earlier, these findings are not exhaustive, particularly in so far as Quebec studies are concerned, and they include little research being performed in disciplines other than economics, history, and political science. Table 1:2 shows the distribution of research activity.

TABLE 1:2

Responses to questionnaire 5 (users) showing geographic location of academics engaged in research in provincial studies and incidence of teaching activity in the field[a]

Province	Quest. sent	Pol. sci. research	Teaching[b]	Economics research	Teaching[b]	History research	Teaching[b]	Total Research	Total Teaching[b]
Nfld.	6	2						2	
NS	21	3 (2)[a]	3	3 (1)	2	3	3	9 (3)	8
PEI	6	(1)		1	1			1 (1)	1
NB	14	2	1	1		1 (2)	1	4 (2)	2
Que.	26	2	1	3	2	4	4	9	7
Ont.	82	12 (1)	15	4	2	7	7	23 (1)	24
Man.	10	1		1				2	
Sask.	4	2		1	1	1		4	2
Alta.	10	2	2	3	3	1	2	6	7
BC	15	1 (3)	1	(4)	3	2	(7)	(14) 4	3
Total	194	27 (7)	24	20 (5)	12	17 (9)	17	64 (21)	54

[a]Figures in brackets indicate additional individuals identified, in interviews, as working in the field.

[b]Number of courses offered dealing wholly or significantly with provincial studies.

Even more suggestive of increasing interest is the recent expansion of teaching activity. Twenty-nine institutions, in eight provinces, reported offering (or definitely proposing to offer) a total of fifty-four courses "dealing wholly or to a significant degree with provincial affairs." Only one of these courses was offered before 1950; four were introduced in the next ten years; nine more in the five years between 1960 and 1965, and the remaining forty have been offered since then, or were to be offered before the end of the 1970-1 academic year.

The strength of interest in the field and the recent proliferation of courses, each in turn capable of exciting still further scholarly involvement, indicates that we are at the beginning of a major expansion in provincial studies. When this fact is considered in conjunction with the growing public need for reliable analyses of provincial affairs, it becomes abundantly clear that Canada's libraries, regardless of the interests they serve, must soon rapidly extend their collections of provincial publications.

For most this will mean that the publications of their own province must be sought out and made available to their users. But for the country's major research libraries, it means a prodigious effort of discovery and acquisition in order to bring their current and retrospective holdings to an acceptable level. What that level should be cannot be defined precisely, but a minimal requirement would see their collections of provincial publications raised to the high standard of completeness now attained by most research libraries for their Canadian, United States, and United Nations holdings.

As we have suggested at the beginning of this chapter, there are five central problems that must be resolved if our libraries are to achieve competence, let alone excellence, in this field.

First, there needs to be a clear definition of a provincial government publication.

Second, we need to rationalize the varied and somewhat haphazard government structures which now exist for processing and distributing provincial publications.

Third, we must establish adequate procedures for the "discovery" of provincial publications.

Fourth, an effective depository system has to be created.

Fifth, we need to devise and introduce workable library procedures for handling provincial publications, including arrangements for reporting and locating documents and for retrieving the information they contain.

NOTES

1 / Professor W.B. Cunningham, Mount Allison University.

2 / This is a conservative estimate. The Manitoba Provincial Library reports that the Manitoba government alone incorporates forty-one reporting agencies.

3 / Ontario Council for the Arts, *Report,* 1967; Ontario Committee on the Aims and Objectives of Education, *Living and Learning,* 1968, and Douglas Sagi, *Globe Magazine,* 29 June 1968,p.3.

4 / See chapter 7.

5 / Adam Shortt and A.G. Doughty, *Canada and Its Provinces* (Toronto: 1913-17, 23 vols.).

6 / For example, Margaret A. Ormsby, *British Columbia: A History* (Toronto: Macmillan, 1958).

7 / The publication of the *Dictionary of Canadian Biography* promises to reduce this need to some extent.

8 / Frank MacKinnon, *The Government of Prince Edward Island* (Toronto: University of Toronto Press, 1951); J.M. Beck, *The Government of Nova Scotia* (Toronto: University of Toronto Press, 1957); M.S. Donnelly, *The Government of Manitoba* (Toronto: University of Toronto Press, 1965). F.F. Schindeler, *Responsible Government in Ontario* (Toronto: University of Toronto Press, 1969) is more limited in scope. Since the above was written, we have learned that S.J.R. Noel's *Politics in Newfoundland* will be published by University of Toronto Press before this work appears.

9 / For example, Hugh G. Thorburn, *Politics in New Brunswick* (Toronto: University of Toronto Press, 1961).

10 / Including the *Dalhousie Review, Ontario History, Saskatchewan History,* and the recently revived *British Columbia Historical Review.*

11 / David Easton, *A Systems Analysis of Political Life* (New York: Wiley, 1965).

12 / Gabriel A. Almond and G. Bingham Powell, Jr., *Comparative Politics: A Developmental Approach* (Boston: Little Brown, 1966).

13 / Many academics commented on the poor quality of the data presented in government publications. Although complaints were made by researchers in all disciplines, economists were most vociferous, pointing out that methods of presenting much data rendered them meaningless and that even where provincial bureaus of economics did exist, the material issued by them originated too frequently in the Dominion Bureau of Statistics.

14 / Motion approved. Minutes, CPSA business meeting, Ottawa, 8 June 1967.

15 / Submission, CPSA to Canada Council, January 1968.

2
Problems of definition: the hidden revolution in information technology

Our need of a new definition of a provincial government publication* has only recently emerged, the by-product of the same changes in copying techniques that have transformed many aspects of publishing. Traditionally, governments easily discriminated between documents enjoying limited, confidential circulation as government records and those destined for mass distribution as publications. The technology of reproduction alone determined this; an item copied four times on a typewriter or even a hundred times on a stencil copier necessarily received a limited circulation. Equally, it was usually thought wasteful to enter into the expense of printing an item if widespread distribution was not intended. As late as 1961, John H. Archer could write: " 'A provincial government document is an original work *printed* for distribution under the authority or with the concourse of that government.' This draws a distinction between government documents and government *records*. The records are the working papers created in the administration of public affairs by a government. They are *not printed*. The *documents* usually arise out of the records, and they *are printed* for distribution. The documents will be of great interest to the librarian; the records will interest the archivist."[1]

Unfortunately this neat distinction is no longer attainable. Many documents, which a few years ago would have been treated as records, are today being reproduced in limited quantities and receiving a small circulation to administrators, consultants, academics, and some libraries. They are government publications.

We do not know why the introduction of the office copier has caused this change, although we can guess at a number of explanations. Perhaps the most

---

*Throughout the study the term "government publication" is used in preference to "government document," the purpose being to avoid the eternal controversy between the archivist and the librarian over the latter term.

important reason, as well as the most obvious, is that a technological innovation generates its own use. Awareness of the office copier's capacity to reproduce documents within a very short time tempts the user to order more copies than he needs. In the words of one government study: "Making copies by means of the electrostatic process has become so quick and easy that people fall into the habit of excessive use and tend to overlook the very substantial costs involved."[2] The study concluded that this technico-psychological factor was the greatest single barrier to reducing photocopying costs, and directed its recommendations accordingly, as the following extract shows:

At the service centres control over the copies ordered will be maintained by using the authorization slip and charge back procedure. *This has value as a psychological safeguard against over-ordering as it involves the possibility of scrutiny and audit. In self-service this is not possible and safeguards can only be made by selecting equipment which minimizes the opportunity for abuse.* The easiest type of equipment to use is the large console type of copier which can produce multiple copies by setting a selecting dial and automatic push button operation. More difficult to operate is the single-shot machine which can produce multiple copies only by reinserting the original and reprocessing the whole cycle. This type of machine demands constant attention to obtain multiple copies and this tends to keep the number of copies made to the minimum required; *it reduces the tendency to produce the extra copy made "just in case."*[3]

There are, however, far more significant ramifications to this technologically induced change in behaviour patterns. Some of these changes affect fundamental relationships between the executive and the administrative and consequently between the public's representatives and the machinery of government. For example, it appears to the authors that the new information technology radically alters communications networks within and around government bureaus, since it makes available to lower-level policy advisers a range of information and an ability to provide information that were formerly the prerogative of only the most senior officials. If we assume that knowledge is power, then we cannot help but conclude that modification of knowledge-diffusing processes is bound to affect bureaucratic power systems and, in turn, the power relationships of government and legislature. To illustrate this point, we need only consider the case of the administrator who elicits outside support for policy proposals by circulating documents to selected professional and interest-group supporters. His action is significant not because it violates traditional rules of administrative secrecy - he has probably done so, orally, for years - but because the use of documents greatly increases the number of participants in the decision-making process and may alter the location at which decisions are actually made.* In other words "documents ... are instruments of policy,"† and policy, as students of the decision-making process have observed, is a function of power.[4] Because of this, it is important to remember that the photocopier is not simply an alternative to the printing press, it is a revolutionary new factor in political communications processes. It is imperative that we revise accordingly our definition of a public document and our procedures for disseminating public information.

These considerations are receiving increasing recognition in the university and library worlds. Although some librarians and academics still believe that the term "government publications" retains its traditional meaning to include only documents such as royal commission reports, legislative papers, agency annual reports, and so on, increasing numbers have become convinced that these are only a part of the materials that should be included in research collections. In Nova Scotia, for example, the Legislative Library has been designated as a depository for all publications "issued or released by a department or agency of the Government for general or *limited* public distribution."[5] At Memorial University of Newfoundland one librarian estimated that 75 per cent of Newfoundland publications that ought to be included in the university collection could be classified as processed documents.[6] ‡ Officials of the Quebec National Library estimate that only 25 per cent of the publications they wish to include in their collection are sold by the Quebec Official Publisher. The remainder, many of them processed documents, have to be obtained from the publishing agencies themselves.[7]

Fundamental to the whole problem is the issue of administrative secrecy, an issue which traditional definitions of government documents conveniently relegated to archivists, officials, journalists, and a few interested academics rather than the librarians and their vast clientele. The intrusion of the readily available processed document has changed all this, raising "not only questions of differential access, but of arbitrary limits to access. The question is not only *who*, but *how many* people are in a position to read such documents."[8] This has forced librarians to confront the issue for the first time and simultaneously pushed the question to the lower administrative ranks. The result has been some difference of opinion amongst librarians, but outright confusion amongst administrators. There seem to be no clear-cut reasons for most officials'

*Should research support the central hypothesis of this paragraph it is quite possible that the technological innovation represented by the common-place office copier will eventually induce some modification of the traditional theory of administrative anonymity. We wish to emphasize that we do not suggest that administrators have not sought outside support in the past, simply that available communications techniques limited the extent of this activity. Today that limitation no longer exists.

†The words of a senior provincial official. The point is treated at greater length in chapter 4.

‡For the purposes of this study a processed document is any document reproduced in quantity by any means other than a typewritten stencil or a lead-type press.

decisions concerning releases of processed documents. An item denied the researcher in one office may be thrust upon him in the next. One man may refuse to release a document containing data readily available in half a dozen annual reports; another may volunteer materials reflecting ongoing policy discussions. Amongst many administrators troubled by this problem, the debate opened by Professor Rowat is being carried on with some intensity.[9] For this reason alone, it is worthwhile to precede an attempt to revise the current definition of a government publication by stating our own view of the administrative secrecy question and relating it to the situation in provincial government publishing.

Briefly, the authors agree with Professor Rowat that Canadian governments should adopt the principle "everything is public unless it is made secret." Like him, too, however, because this principle runs counter to every cherished tenet of Canadian administration, we recognize that the most we can hope for in the immediate future is limited progress towards its adoption.

Effective administration depends upon efficient communication between all segments of the political system. Our technological culture is particularly dependent on its various mechanisms for transmitting and translating information between segments. Somehow political and administrative decision-makers must absorb and act upon an infinite range of technical and scientific information while simultaneously ensuring that the public has at least a minimal understanding of the effort made on its behalf. This is, of course, the contemporary version of the traditional problem of sustaining a healthy democracy through an informed public, a problem amply explored by more able discussants. We shall only note that the professionalism and technological sophistication of the modern administrator necessarily interposes a barrier to communication, not only with the public at large, but with the press and those traditionally assigned responsibility for interest aggregation and articulation, the politicians.[10] To overcome this problem, agencies normally adopt the strategy of appointing information officers who vainly attempt to substitute a pleasant and helpful manner for genuine elucidation of problems. Some have founded,[11] or encouraged, sympathetic pressure groups to provide sufficient external demand to sustain administratively desired innovations.

These strategies have had very limited success and it seems clear that governments must find more effective alternatives if they are to avoid the extensive communications failures which, Harold Innis has argued, crippled earlier political systems.[12] One alternative is to allow greater freedom to the relatively independent forces - the interested private citizens, the journalists, and the academics - who are capable of acting as middlemen in the process of translating felt needs into clearly articulated demands.

This is not a novel proposition. Such communications roles have been observed by students of transitional societies who have argued that "the emergence of critical elements throughout the societies who have a sense of competence and who are dedicated to raising the level of society"[13] are crucial to the proper functioning of viable democratic institutions. In developed countries, too, journalists, citizens, and academics, as well as politicians and pressure groups, have traditionally been involved in the process of articulating public demands and translating government positions and capabilities to the public. In our view, however, journalists, private citizens, and academics have been able to play only a very limited part in the process because they have not been allowed access to the information they need to form rational judgments. Academics have been particularly limited because their information requirements are much more extensive than those of journalists and usually of private citizens. Many of us, including the authors, have had to observe unnecessary and sometimes unfair restrictions limiting the use of data collected. Worse, fear of reprisal has made us reluctant to criticize governmental, and particularly administrative, activity. The journal *Canadian Public Administration,* for example, is particularly void of constructive criticism. Such practices are destructive of scholarship and eventually of the political system itself.

If the process of political communication is to be improved, measures must be taken to ensure that more information with fewer restrictions reaches the middlemen. The means to achieve this end are threefold. The first, ease of dissemination of data, has been provided by the technological revolution in copying. The second is the achievement of a suitably broad definition of a government publication. The third is the creation of structures charged with ensuring that necessary information reaches the public and its middlemen.

There is no need to elaborate further the impact of the copying revolution, and we can turn immediately to the question of definition.

The federal government defines a government publication as any printed material issued by a department *except:*

(a) business forms, which include any documents with blank spaces for the insertion of information, used to secure or convey data, either within the government or from the public, such as letterheads, envelopes ... ;

(b) administrative instructions, reports and other materials for the internal use of a department; or issued by central agencies to the departments;

(c) blue-printing and photocopying;

(d) complimentary, visiting and business cards ... ;

(e) press releases, clip-sheets, speeches and other printed matter produced for the use of news media;

(f) items such as excise, postage ... stamps ... ;

(g) maps and charts ... ;

(h) catalogues produced by the National Gallery ... ;

(i) library bindings;

(j) correspondence;

(k) engineering orders and manuals of instruction used by the Department of National Defence.[14]

This is too restrictive a definition; photocopied material is, as we have pointed out, frequently far more interesting to the library user than the printed emanations of governments. The same is true of materials prepared for the news media, and even maps and catalogues. Conversely the only definition included in the United States act relating to public printing and documents is so broad that it is nebulous: " 'Government publication' ... means informational matter which is published as an individual document at Government expense, or as required by law."[15]

We suggest that *a government publication is created when a document prepared by or for an agency of government is reproduced and circulated to individuals and groups other than those advising or negotiating with the government concerning the subject matter of the document.* This is an inverted "need to know" formula; if an official or private citizen has access to documents he does not need in order to carry on some formal relationship with government, then the documents in question should be available to other members of the public. The range of documents covered by this definition is extremely broad. Everything from a tourist map to a limited circulation economic study may be included. Necessarily so; one man's ephemera is another's life work, and issuing agencies should leave the task of discriminating between desirable and undesirable acquisitions to the librarian and the user.

Thus, a publication is defined not by the process by which it is reproduced, but by the breadth of circulation accorded it. Its circulation beyond the immediate confines of a government and those advising or doing business with authority removes a document from the status of record, and thus the concern of the records manager and the archivist, to the status of publication, and the purview of the general public and the librarian.

Without denying the need to establish a definition, at the moment the creation of a responsibility centre is really far more important. For until a specific administrator has been given the duty and incentive to apply classification rules in an equitable fashion, it is unlikely that any number of definitions will ensure that the necessary documents are made available to the general public. Furthermore, procedures must exist that will ensure that such an administrator does in fact see all the potential publications produced by his government and has the opportunity to apply classification standards to them. Finally, machinery will be needed to place on the shelves of depository libraries all documents, including the most esoteric processed items, judged to be public in character.

The measures necessary to achieve these aims will be outlined in a later chapter. In the meantime it is encouraging to note that the proliferation of reproduction facilities may make it possible for the "middlemen" to perform their roles more effectively. It is also important that this factor has forced a wider discussion of the issue of administrative secrecy. It is discouraging to find, however, that some Canadian governments hold the view that government publishing is essentially a public relations operation. In the words of one treasury board publication:

Government publications are a means of promoting the effectiveness of departmental policies and programs by (a) enlisting public co-operation for these policies and programs ...; (b) encouraging immigration and tourism; (c) making available abroad information ... ; (d) promoting the use of ... products ... (e) disseminating the results of technical, scientific, economic, statistical or historical studies; and (f) providing information to the public in answer to requests, in order to protect health and welfare, to assist in education or training and to meet emergencies.[16]

It is information, not propaganda, that we must aim to place on library shelves.

NOTES

1 / "Acquisition of Canadian Provincial Government Documents," *Library Resources and Technical Services*, V, 1 (Winter, 1961). Our italics.

2 / Confidential source.

3 / *Ibid*. Our italics. Quite apart from the "just in case" syndrome there is considerable temptation to use this new resource. Data can be quickly prepared for circulation within agencies and within segments of the general public; individual officials can obtain a wider audience for research memoranda, both within and beyond the agency. A variety of human motivations, ranging from career to policy promotion can be seen as contributing to the extensive use now made of the office copier. For example, one Treasury Board official was highly suspicious of the motives leading to the publication of much material, pointing out that much may originate simply because ambitious young men wish to attract attention. This is similar to the use of classification referred to by O'Rourke (*Secrecy and Publicity: Dilemmas of Democracy*, Baltimore: Johns Hopkins, 1966, 80) whereby the ambitious official over-classifies his reports in the hopes that they will more readily reach the most senior members of his agency. In the provincial example, the junior official seeks to broaden the base of his influence.

4 / See W.J. Gore, *Administrative Decision-Making: A Heuristic Model* (New York, Wiley, 1964).

5 / *Nova Scotia Management Manual*, Bulletin 109-31, 17 January 1967. Our italics.

6 / Interview with P. Rahal.

7 / Interview with M.P. Marcoux.

8 / I.L. Horowitz, "Social Science and Public Policy," *International Studies Quarterly*, XI, 1 (March 1967), 32-62, 48.

9 / See D. Rowat, "How Much Administrative Secrecy," *Canadian Journal of Economics and Political Science*, XXXI, 4 (November 1965), 479-99; K.W. Knight, "Administrative Secrecy and Ministerial Responsibility," and D.C. Rowat, "Administrative Secrecy and Ministerial Responsibility: A Reply," *Canadian Journal of Economics and Political Science*, XXXII, 1 (February 1966), 77-88; A.S. Abel, "Administrative Secrecy," and Jacques Premont, "Publicité de documents officiels," *Canadian Public Administration*, XI, 4 (Winter, 1968), 440-54.

10 / A.P. Pross has noted the emergence of this problem in the Ontario Department of Lands and Forests where a predominantly professional department has had increasing difficulty communicating with the public, as the recent debate over Algonquin Park and the attempt to divide the Department have shown. See *The Development of a Forest Policy: A Study of the Ontario Department of Lands and Forests* (University of Toronto, unpublished PhD thesis, 1967) esp. 321-2.

11 / This aspect of the policy process was suggested by J.E. Hodgetts who has observed that departments of agriculture have superintended the creation of several farmers' groups. Antony A. Adamson recently told members of the Community Planning Association of Canada that the organization "was called into being by government subsidy as stooges of the government to sell town planning to the inexpert." *Civic Administration* (June 1970) 2.

12 / H.A. Innis, "Minerva's Owl" in *The Bias of Communication* (Toronto: University of Toronto Press, 1951). Our assumption that communications strategies have had limited success and the ensuing prophecy are, of course, highly debatable, and A.P. Pross plans to pursue the question further in a forthcoming publication.

13 / Lucian W. Pye, *Communications and Political Development* (Princeton, NJ: Princeton University Press, 1965), esp. 58-63.

14 / Canada, Treasury Board, *Policy and Guide on Canadian Government Publishing* (Ottawa: Treasury Board, processed, 1967), 1.

15 / 44 USC, "Public Printing and Documents," s. 1901.

16 / Canada, Treasury Board, *Policy and Guide*, 13.

3
The current model for production

The nineteen-sixties witnessed an extraordinary expansion in the production of provincial government publications. In every area of provincial administration the quantity and variety of documents demanded by and thrust upon the public has increased. Such expansion has posed serious problems not only for the librarian and the scholar, but also for the Queen's Printer, traditionally responsible for government printing, financial officers concerned about mounting costs, and the agencies which issue them.[1]

A variety of reasons for this growth are advanced by those most concerned with the problem. Widening public awareness of the literature available, improvements in content and presentation of material, larger populations, industrial expansion, and departmental promotion of literature have all been suggested. Spill-over from the success of the federal Queen's Printer might also account for part of the growth, and the expansion of government activity, requiring, as it does, greater public awareness of government action, would also be a factor. Certain aspects of administrative behaviour account for some expansion; individuals and their departments frequently seek to promote themselves through the medium of publication. But it is possible that one of the least considered causes of expansion may be one of the most important. Today, as never before, equipment for inexpensive volume reproduction is readily available. Many departments of government, in addition to placing small photo-copiers in individual offices, have found that it is economical to bypass traditional governmental publishing structures by buying their own equipment capable of achieving volume copying at high speed.

There have been two principal effects of this latter development on government publishing in the provinces. On the one hand, it has accelerated a previously existing tendency towards increased volume of production. On the other hand, it has challenged established administrative structures concerned with government printing and publishing. Both results have had their impact on distribution procedures and, since it is difficult to conceive of a solution to distribution problems without some settlement of the difficulties occurring on the production side, both results merit some intensive investigation.

Widespread introduction of copying equipment cannot account for all increased volume; many of the items referred to have been printed on commercial or governmental printing presses. Nevertheless, examination of the types of publication currently available and of the procedural steps leading to publication suggests that the presence of copying equipment has contributed greatly to this development.

Generally, provincial government publications can be divided into two categories; (1) statutory publications (often referred to as "official") and (2) non-statutory publications ("departmental," "administrative," or "unofficial"). The importance and role of statutory publications can be traced to public belief in the principle of rule of law. Demands that the public be kept informed of government action have ensured, to a varying extent, the systematic, official publication of certain documents. Depending on the jurisdiction, statutory provision for publication of documents can cover as broad a field as (1) the provincial *Gazette*, (2) provincial statutes and regulations, (3) legislative documents such as debates or journals, or both, (4) departmental annual reports, (5) departmental estimates, and (6) provincial public accounts. Usually, however, only the statutes, the *Gazette*, and consolidations of statutes and regulations receive the systematic handling that the term "statutory publication" implies. Their pre-eminent position is due to the fact that laws and regulations cannot be distributed to the public in a vague and haphazard fashion. The courts require that the government speak with a single voice in such matters and, as a result, each provincial government has determined that a specific official, usually the Queen's Printer, shall be responsible for publishing statutory documents and that "all copies of proclamations, official and other notices, advertisements, and documents printed in *The Royal Gazette* and all copies of the statutes of the Province printed for the Government by the Queen's Printer, shall be *prima facie* evidence of the originals."[2] Table 3:1 provides details of the provisions made for this type of publication in the public printing act of each of the provinces.[3]

As Table 3:1 suggests, publication procedure for documents other than statutes and gazettes varies considerably. Thus, for example, in Prince Edward Island legislative papers are processed by the stenographic staff of the Clerk of the Assembly, while some departments prefer to mimeograph the relatively small runs of regulations they require, and these consequently do not pass through the hands of the Queen's Printer.[4] In New Brunswick the Synoptic Reports of the Legislature were printed under the authority of the Queen's Printer until recently, when the Clerk of the Assembly undertook direct responsibility for their publication and distribution on a daily basis.[5] Table 3:2 shows the procedures reported in each province.

Non-statutory documents do not depend on the authority of the Queen's

TABLE 3:1

*Statutory provision for
publication by Queen's Printer*

Province	Authority	Documents to be published
Nfld.	RSN (1952) c.27, s.10	statutes, *Newfoundland Gazette* and "all such official and Departmental and other reports, forms, documents, commissions, and other papers as he is required to cause to be printed and published by or under the authority of the Lieutenant-Governor in Council."
PEI	RSPEI (1951) c.1, s.23(5), c.2, s.15	*Royal Gazette*, revised statutes
NS	RSNS (1967) c.252, s.3(1)	*Royal Gazette*, statutes, journals, "and all such official, departmental and other reports, books, forms, documents and other papers as are required to be printed at the expense of the province."
NB	*Statutes of New Brunswick* (1961-2) c.28, s.1(4)	*Royal Gazette*, statutes, journals, "and all such official, departmental and other reports, books, forms, documents and other papers as are required to be printed by law at the expense of the province."
Que.	RSQ (1964) c.54, s.22	*Quebec Official Gazette*, statutes, "such documents and announcements as the Lieutenant-Governor in Council may require to be printed or published."
Ont.	RSO (1960) c.383, s.6; c.266, s.1	*Ontario Gazette*, statutes
Man.	RSM (1954) c.214, ss.8, 10	*Manitoba Gazette*, statutes, office consolidations, votes and proceedings of the assembly, orders of the day of the assembly, journals of the assembly, public accounts of the province, "such other publications as the Provincial Secretary may prescribe."
Sask.	RSS (1965) c.46 s.4, 9(2)	statutes, *Saskatchewan Gazette*, "such documents and announcements as may from time to time be required," journals of the legislature, sessional papers
Alta.	RSA (1955) c.275, s.4	*Alberta Gazette*, statutes, "such documents and announcements as may be required from time to time."
BC	RSBC (1960) c.318, ss.6(1), 8	*British Columbia Gazette*, "Acts, Journals, Sessional Papers, and other printed documents placed before the Legislature ..."

TABLE 3:2

Duties of the Queen's Printers:
data from questionnaires 1 (Queen's Printers) and 2 (government departments)

Type of document	Carries out all work other than manuscript preparation	Queen's Printer calls for tenders from private firms, awards contracts	Prints documents on government equipment
statutes	Que., NB	NS, Man., PEI Sask.[d]	BC, Alta., Nfld., Ont.
gazette	Que., NB	NS, Man., Sask.[d]	BC, PEI, Alta., Nfld., Ont.
legislative papers (bills, order paper, but not debates)	NB	NS, Sask.[d]	BC, Man., Ont.
debates		Sask.[d]	NS, Man.
journals		NS, Man., PEI, NB, Sask.[d]	Ont.
departmental reports		NS[a], Man.[a], Que., PEI[d], NB, Sask.[d], Ont.[e]	NS[a], BC, Man.[a], Alta.[a], PEI[a]
departmental regulations	NB	NS[a], Man.[a], Que., PEI[a], Sask.[d]	NS[a], BC, Alta.[a], PEI[a].
other departmental publications		Man.[a], PEI[a], NB, Sask.[d]	BC, Man.[a], Alta.[a], PEI[a].
reports of boards & commissions		Man.[c], Que., PEI[a], NB, Sask.	NS[a], BC, Alta.[a]
regulations of boards & commissions	NB	Man.[b], NS[a], Que., Sask.[d]	NS[a], BC, Alta.[a]
royal commission reports		Man.[a], Que., PEI[a], NB, Sask.[d]	NS, BC, Man.[a], Alta.[a], PEI[a]

Symbols:

a   practice varies
b   gazette
c   Public Utilities Commission, Civil Service Commission, Municipal Board; others are independent of Queen's Printer
d   awards contracts
e   recommends awards

24 / GOVERNMENT PUBLISHING IN THE CANADIAN PROVINCES

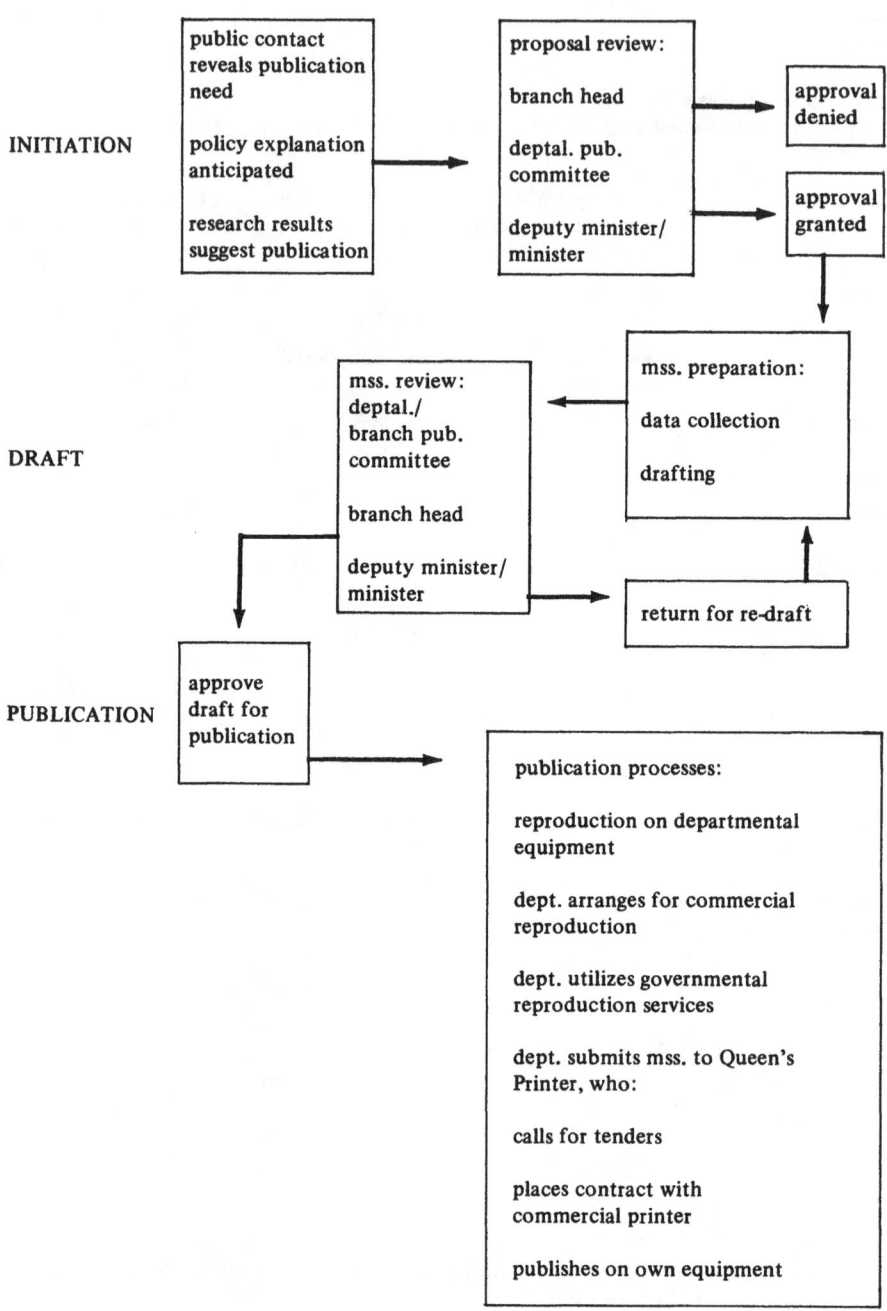

CHART 3:1 The stages of production

Printer's imprimatur for recognition, and they are not demanded by the legislature. Instead they originate in departments' needs to inform the public concerning matters within their jurisdiction. Often the public printing act provides only vague directions for the publication procedure that must be applied to them; the Quebec act, for example, provides that the Quebec Official Publisher shall process only "such official documents as the Lieutenant-Governor in Council may require."[6] Consequently, many departments possess considerable latitude in determining what method of production will be used in the case of each non-statutory publication. In order to clarify the number of options available to publishing departments, an attempt has been made in the accompanying flow chart and in the explanation that follows, to describe all the various steps involved in the production of such a publication. While the flow chart represents only a "model" of production, and thus a generalization rather than an existing structure, it is hoped that the picture presented is close enough to reality to assist the librarian anxious to discover the source of a publication and to provide the general reader with a more specific view of the production process and thus a clearer idea of the difficulties of controlling and directing the course of production.

The initial proposal that a departmental publication should be prepared tends to originate in one of three situations. First, and possibly most frequent, the department becomes aware, through staff contact with the public, that a demand exists for certain types of information. This practice was reported most frequently by departments of agriculture, where the field service performs a communication function that is particularly important to departmental operations, but it also occurs in trade and industry departments and probably is found frequently in natural resource and public welfare agencies. A second point of origin is the decision to explain departmental policy to the public, a decision that might flow from a feedback process such as that described above, or simply from anticipation of public need. Literature of the type describing New Brunswick's "Program for Equal Opportunity" would fall into this second category. Finally, much government literature originates in research organizations and may report research findings unrelated to any specific demand input or withinput. It will be noted that this list has not included initiation of publications by the executive. While such initiation exists, research suggests that policy decisions related to specific publications are generally initiated at the middle to upper management level of departments concerned and reach the ministerial level only when a final decision must be taken concerning continuation or cessation of a publishing project. Similarly, there appears to be little interdepartmental communication concerning publications, even when the subject matter of a publication concerns more than one department;[7] decentralization at this level has resulted in considerable duplication of material.

Once the publication procedure has been initiated, no standard pattern of activity exists. As a general rule, however, departments with extensive publishing programs exhibit the most elaborate structures for reviewing proposals leading to publication and usually delegate publication policy formulation to lower levels of the organization than do departments with less ambitious publishing programs. Thus, for example, in the government of Prince Edward Island, which is reported to issue about seventy-five publications a year,[8] a typical publication might have the following production history. Once a proposal to produce a publication has been approved, at the ministerial level, preparation of a manuscript is usually undertaken by the department's experts in the subject area of the publication and a finished draft submitted to the minister and deputy minister. Following final approval of the manuscript, the deputy minister will requisition the Queen's Printer to print a specified number of copies. The Queen's Printer will in turn assign the order to a commercial printer if the government press cannot be used for the job. When an outside printer is employed, the Queen's Printer may consult the department before making a final selection. After the work is completed the printer, if a commercial printer is employed, delivers the print order to the department but sends the invoice, with two samples of the work, to the Queen's Printer whose approval must be obtained before payment can be made from the appropriation of the department concerned.[9] A more elaborate procedure is found in the British Columbia Department of Agriculture. There each branch of the department formally proposes a publication, when it reaches manuscript stage, to a departmental publications committee. The committee, which from time to time also initiates publications, checks for style and content and then initiates the reproduction procedure.[10]

Before examining this latter procedure it is worth noting that in all the provincial governments there exists virtually no machinery to control or co-ordinate any part of this pre-publication activity. In only one jurisdiction, Alberta, has an office been established to provide departments with assistance in the publishing area. Alberta's operation, the Alberta Publicity Bureau, is a central agency engaged in preparing publicity items, often taking a publication through from an idea put forward by a department to manuscript stage and thence to printed product. On occasion the Bureau also distributes materials for other agencies.[11] The Bureau's work is highly specialized, however. It is essentially carrying out a public relations function and is not equipped to co-ordinate the production of all provincial publications. Given the nature of the Bureau's present assignment, the extension of its role would be far from desirable, even if the various departments most concerned could be persuaded to exchange what is now a voluntary relationship for an obligatory one. A similar but more satisfactory co-ordinating device has been proposed in Ontario and will be discussed below.

Once the decision to publish has been taken, the department finds that it has a wide variety of options available. In the case of the British Columbia Department of Agriculture, for example, the department can use the resources of its Publications Branch, the Queen's Printer, or a commercial printer, if the latter can show that he can carry out the jobs more cheaply.[12] In a very small number of cases, such as that of the Farm Economics, Crops and Statistics Branch of the Ontario Department of Agriculture, all the work of preparing, reproducing, and distributing documents can take place within the branch itself.[13] Our flow chart suggests four options open to the department:

Option 1: The Department could maintain its own reproduction equipment. As has been suggested, this is a fairly common procedure. Over-all figures are not available, but only two provinces, New Brunswick and Manitoba, claimed to have effectively centralized reproduction facilities. In New Brunswick the central duplicating section of the Department of Public Works performs this function.[14] In Manitoba the Queen's Printer's office claims that departmental operation of copying equipment is rare and 99 per cent of governmental copying work required in the city of Winnipeg is done in one of the four Queen's Printer's shops in the city.[15] In the other provinces departmental possession and operation of equipment is more common, varying principally with the wealth of the province, reaching its greatest extent in Ontario, where a recent study showed that twenty-two printing shops (for offset printing only) were being operated within the government,[16] a figure that has since been halved[17] but does not include photo-copiers installed in most departments.

Option 2: Departmental arrangement for printing by commercial printer. Although most governments centralize procedures for distributing contracts to commercial firms, there are jurisdictions in which a higher degree of latitude is permitted. Thus five of twenty respondents to the question, "To what extent is your department concerned with the production of the government documents issued?"[18] replied that their departments were responsible for all phases of publications, including the awarding of printing contracts. The fact that in some cases this response clashed with that of the Queen's Printer of the province illustrates the lack of order that pervades the field of provincial government publication. Only in one province, New Brunswick, has the Queen's Printer followed a policy of dissociation from commercial printing of non-statutory documents. There, the Queen's Printer Act now provides that the Queen's Printer is required to print only such documents "as are required to be printed *by Law.*"[19] This leaves departments free to select their own publisher or to have the work carried out by the central duplicating division of the Department of Public Works. Here again, however, there appears to be some disparity in practice, with one department (Agriculture) reporting that all printing requisitions have to be channelled through the purchasing section of the Department of Public Works, whilst the Queen's Printer and another department reported a lack of central control. In Alberta printing requisitions are supposed to be channelled through the Queen's Printer or, where a publicity item is concerned, through the Publicity Bureau. In fact, one official maintained that this requirement is not always observed.

Option 3: Department arranges for publication by governmental reproduction services. Central reproduction facilities exist in all the provinces and are attached to the Departments of Public Works in New Brunswick, Quebec, and Ontario; the Queen's Printer in Prince Edward Island, Nova Scotia, Manitoba, Alberta, and British Columbia; the Department of Supply in Newfoundland; and the Office Services Division of the Saskatchewan Government Purchasing Agency. Centralization produces both advantages and disadvantages. The disadvantages are such that Treasury officials in at least three provinces took pains to discourage any proposals leading to centralization of production and distribution of provincial publications. Quoting the *Glassco Report*[20] to the effect that diminution of responsibility entails diminution of accountability, they argue that centralization should be introduced only when "excellent reasons" are put forward. A typical example of the evils of centralization was provided by a Manitoba official, who reported that "the line-up for service got very long. [They] argued with everyone who went down. Getting our own equipment meant we can produce more quickly what we need and on time. The personality of the people [there] is not conducive to efficiency. Operational necessities are of only secondary importance to central service people. They find quickly that people are dependent on them and take advantage of the fact to 'get back' at people above [whom] they resent." The Manitoba experience is not unique, but the costs of decentralization worry Treasury officials, including those who dislike centralization. The Saskatchewan Office Services Division represents a compromise: a policy of operational decentralization is combined with an attitude of "gentle persuasion." Provided with equipment in several locations convenient to user departments, the division operates on the principles (a) that departments should be required to use Office Services only if they obviously cannot use their own equipment economically and (b) that the departments should be sold a service, not required to submit to centralization. The division maintains that its ability to provide fast, cheap service has convinced several departments to give up their own reproduction facilities.[21] The newly established Central Duplicating Service of the Ontario Department of Public Works is reported to rest on a similar principle.[22]

Option 4: Department publishes material through the Queen's Printer. As has been suggested, this fourth option is decreasingly acceptable to departments, a factor that has upset the traditional authority structure involving the Queen's Printer. Although historical data are inadequate to show the reasons for the original establishment of the Queen's Printer, several reasons are frequently suggested. First, governments met the need to indicate that certain documents have the full authority of the government by designating one printer as the King or Queen's Printer. This point has been discussed. Second, as governments extended their publishing activities, it was thought that centralizing responsibility would be more economical. Third, it was argued that the Queen's Printer would also have the function of ensuring the probity of printing contracts through the procedure of calling for tenders. The validity of this argument has never been proven. Fourth, increased printing activity led some governments to consider the "make-or-buy" question and drew them to the conclusion that the government should "make" and should establish a full-fledged printing plant to carry out all government printing. A rationalization sometimes provided where such a system has been adopted is the view that the confidential nature of some government printing demands that it be produced on government presses.[23] However, at least one study has discounted this theory, arguing that "the confidential nature of some government material has very little bearing on the make-or-buy question."[24]

Three patterns of development were followed by provincial governments. At one extreme, the Newfoundland case, the Queen's Printer is a commercial company designated Queen's Printer by virtue of the fact that it prints the provincial statutes and the *Newfoundland Gazette*. Other printing assignments carried out for the Newfoundland government are executed by this and other publishing firms. The task of awarding contracts, warehousing publications, and meeting some public requests usually undertaken by a Queen's Printer rests with the Department of Supply.[25]

In several provinces (Nova Scotia, New Brunswick, Quebec, Ontario, and Manitoba) the Queen's Printer is primarily responsible for advertising and awarding contracts and ensuring that they are properly fulfilled. He is described as "a purchasing printer. He doesn't see himself giving assistance on how to assemble a document, cataloguing documents, carrying supplies to provide for requests."[26] Sometimes these agencies have little or nothing to do with actually handling the documents concerned. More often the Queen's Printer and his staff are professional printers whose experience is used to provide typographic and costing advice.

Finally, in the other provinces (Prince Edward Island, Alberta, Saskatchewan, and British Columbia) the Queen's Printer is a full-fledged printer running an elaborate printing plant which includes standard printing and copying equipment. Despite the extent of these operations, only one claims to be capable of handling all the work generated by the government. The exception is the Queen's Printer of British Columbia, who points out that commercial printers may do government work if they can do so more cheaply than his operation. A commercial costing system has been in use since 1954 and the operation apparently maintains a high degree of efficiency as outside printers do not carry out a great deal of work for the government.[27] Elsewhere, however, the Queen's Printer shares a high proportion of the workload with commercial printers[28] and in Saskatchewan a recent highly critical Royal Commission report has argued that the present system is uneconomical and has urged that the province buy the bulk of its printing under an estimate and tender system.[29]

It is the Queen's Printers who have been most prone to dispute with departments over publishing jurisdictions. The chief bone of contention has been copying equipment, and Queen's Printers have attacked departmental installations on the grounds of expense and the fact that they infringe the established jurisdictional structure. Thus, in 1964, prior to the most expansive period of growth in the copying equipment field, the Alberta Queen's Printer pointed out that various government agencies other than the Queen's Printer possessed thirty-four machines and urged that

Some of the operations if not consolidated in the Queen's Printer's plant, should be placed under the direct supervision of the Queen's Printer to ensure the utmost economy, and in fact, to assess the advisability of discontinuing operation by the departments. If this equipment is used only part time (and I am sure it is in many cases), it would be wise to move the equipment into the Queen's Printer's building where it would be used to full advantage ... I feel sure savings could be effected by adopting this suggestion."[30]

A similar complaint was expressed by a representative of the British Columbia Queen's Printer who argued that departmental installations "represent unnecessary duplication and their costs tend to be hidden as departments claim their normal office staff can handle the work."[31] In New Brunswick even though the Queen's Printer has relinquished some degree of control over non-official publications (e.g., travel bureau material) he would like to see all printing come under control of his office. He feels that if the Queen's Printer had charge of all printing it would save a considerable amount as he would be able to allot contracts in the most economical fashion.[32]

The plea of jurisdictional infringement arouses little sympathy at the highest policy-making level. Departments have been able to argue, with some success, that centralized printing and reproduction services do not meet their needs and in fact inhibit the efficient performance of departmental responsibilities. Policy-makers are sensitive, however, to the charge that departmental printing activities have quietly grown out of control. In several provinces officials are carrying out enquiries into departmental publishing and are in the process of formulating new policy alternatives. In Alberta, a Treasury Department study asked all departments to compile lists of all publications issued in 1967, specifying who printed the document, the number of copies printed, how they were distributed and the total cost of the publication, together with the charge, if any, to the public. The study is chiefly concerned with inconsistencies in criteria for what is to be published, how publications are distributed and the charges to be made for publications.[33] Although the study has not yet been completed, early findings pointed to the high costs of duplicating limited edition items on photocopying machines. This is corroborated by a confidential study in another province which suggests that non-optimum use of equipment has added considerably to department publishing costs. Investigation has not been limited to the problems posed by installation of copying equipment. Treasury officials sometimes claim that departments hide publishing costs or embark on publication projects without establishing costs. The following illustrates this point:

> The 1966-67 estimates for the Department ... show only $4,000 provided for the publication of ... It is estimated that over $15,000 has actually been spent to date, including printing, binding, and advertising.
> In 1967-68 only $2,100 is provided in the estimates. Because work will begin on the first supplement as well as continue on the original unit, actual costs should exceed the $15,000 level experienced in 1966-67.[34]

It was estimated that this item would cost the taxpayer $4.00 per copy in addition to the substantial price paid by each purchaser. When it is remembered that such costs are not unusual - $12 to $15 a copy is frequently the cost of a departmental annual report - the reasons for government concern can be readily understood.

There are only limited options available to policy-makers bent on reducing these costs. In today's world, where public understanding and discussion of a policy is increasingly dependent on the abilities of journalist and academic middlemen, curtailing publication is infeasible. In theory, much can be achieved through centralization of publishing services, but as has been suggested, such a policy must be approached with caution and a full understanding of the dangers. In the words of one official, "you can't impose a system of document control without basing it on good will. You immediately challenge people to either avoid it or overwhelm it."[35]

Only one jurisdiction, Ontario,[36] has attempted to create a complete publishing policy. Its plan, instituted between 1968 and 1970, envisaged the Department of Public Works as responsible for providing duplicating or printing services for all departments in the Queen's Park complex whilst "the Department of the Provincial Secretary and Citizenship [would] provide a central service for the establishment and maintenance of quality standards for government publications ... An experienced publications executive [was to] be appointed as Queen's Publisher to head up this operation and to provide advice and assistance with a view to achieving a uniformly high standard of editorial content of all government publications."[37] The theory behind the proposal is similar to that of the Saskatchewan Office Services Division: "The answer to departmental complaints about the level of service is to make sure no one gets worse service and many get better service. The departments can opt out, but they will have to come to Treasury Board for new equipment and will have to bring detailed costs with them. This will provide a great challenge to the manager of central services and it avoids the tendency to use the central service as a whipping boy."[38] The success of the operation will depend on its ability to convince users of its desirability. Unfortunately it has not been possible to assess the effectiveness of the new operation, since the newly appointed Ontario Queen's Printer and Publisher has not been available for interviews and has not responded to written enquiries. It is known, however, that the office has been located entirely in the Department of Public Works rather than partially in the Provincial Secretary's Department as originally intended. It is to be hoped that the new arrangement will prove successful since it holds out the hope of vastly improving the co-ordination of production, quality of publication, and methods of distribution.

NOTES

1 / Although the vast majority of those interviewed commented on the rising flood of provincial publications, data were not available proving conclusively that production has accelerated in recent years. Opinion differs sharply amongst both librarians and administrators, partly because of differing views of what constitutes a publication. In general, interviews with administrators suggested that an increase in the variety of provincial publications has taken place. Of the fourteen respondents to question 6(b) of questionnaire 2 (government departments), twelve reported that "demand for publications has increased in recent years," while two reported no increase. Increased demand does not necessarily entail increased production and few agencies supplied figures to support their assertion. Of those supplying such figures, the Alberta Department of Agriculture reported that demand has jumped from 232,000 items to 393,000 items between 1966 and 1968. The increase is attributed to a reorganization of publications procedures in the department. *The New Brunswick Economic Statistics* has a print run of 650 copies, up 500 since it was first published. Saskatchewan Department of Agriculture technical bulletins are reported to have found an increased demand in recent years; both Departments of Education and Agriculture in Ontario reported increased demand.

In August 1970, after the above was written, the National Library of Canada reported that about 8,000 new provincial documents had been listed in *Canadiana* since 1968. "There has been a tremendous increase in the amount of material coming from Quebec and Ontario and slight increases from other provinces. Coverage has probably improved in many provinces." Letter J.P. Bourque, Chief, Government Publications Division, National Library of Canada, to A.P. Pross, 26, Aug. 1970.

2 / "The Queen's Printer Act," *RSNB* (1952), c.189, s.10. Although specific reference is not made to all the documents of a statutory nature published in each province, the public printing act always makes specific reference to the statutes and the *Gazette*. See: "Queen's Printer Act," *RSA* (1955), c.275, s.4; "The Public Printing Act," *RSBC* (1960), c.318, ss.6(1), 8; "The Public Printing Act," *RSM* (1954), c.214, ss.8, 10; "An Act to Amend the Queen's Printer Act," Statutes of New Brunswick (1961-2), c.28, s.1(4); "The Public Printing and Stationery Act," *RSN* (1952), c.27, s.10(1); "The Public Printing Act," *RSNS* (1967), c.252, s.3(1); "The Interpretation Act," *RSPEI* (1951), c.1, s.23(5) and "The Revised Statutes Act," *RSPEI*, c.2, s.15; "The Statutes Act," *RSO* (1960), c.383, s.6, and "The Official Notices Publication Act," *RSO*, c.266, s.1; "Provincial Secretary's Department Act," *RSQ* (1964), c.54, s.22; "An Act to Amend the Provincial Secretary's Department Act," Bill 71, Legislative Assembly of Quebec, 3rd Session, 28th Legislature (1968); "The Queen's Printer Act," *RSS* (1965), c.46, ss.4, 9(2).

3 / A complete listing of all the documents required by statute to be published is available only for Manitoba, where one has been prepared for the Legislative Assembly.

THE CURRENT MODEL FOR PRODUCTION / 33

4 / Interview with Mr D. Boylan, Legislative Librarian, Prince Edward Island.
5 / Interview with Mr W.A. Peterson, Queen's Printer, NB.
6 / *RSQ* (1964), c.54, s.22.
7 / Interviews. Especially interviews with A.D. O'Brien, Department of Provincial Treasurer, Alberta, and H.E. Martin, Director of Publicity and Advertising, Publicity Bureau, Government of Alberta.
8 / Interview with Mr D. Boylan.
9 / Description based on interviews with Mr. L. C. Wright, Deputy Minister of Agriculture, and with the Queen's Printer.
10 / Interview with Mr A. Nelson, Field Crops Branch, British Columbia Department of Agriculture.
11 / Interview with Mr H. Martin, Director of Publicity and Advertising, Publicity Bureau, Alberta.
12 / Interviews with Messrs Nelson and Oxendale, BC Department of Agriculture, and Mr K. MacDonald of the Queen's Printer's Office.
13 / Interview with Dr H.S. Patterson, Director.
14 / Interview with Mr W.A. Peterson, Queen's Printer, New Brunswick.
15 / Interview with Mr B.M. Hudson, Queen's Printer's Office.
16 / Interview with Mr D.Y. Lewis, Executive Director of Administration and Finance, Ontario Department of Public Works.
17 / Interview with Mr J.G. O'Neill, Executive Director, Advisory Services Division, Treasury Board, Ontario.
18 / Questionnaire 2, question 1.
19 / *NBS* (1961-2), c.28, s.1(4).
20 / Royal Commission on Government Organization (Ottawa, Queen's Printer).
21 / Interview with Mr R. Borrowman, Director of Purchases, Saskatchewan Purchasing Agency.
22 / Interview with Mr D.Y. Lewis, Executive Director of Administration and Finance, Ontario Department of Public Works.
23 / When the Alberta plant was established in the 1930s it seemed mainly concerned with confidential material. Interview with Mr L.S. Wall, Queen's Printer.
24 / *Saskatchewan Royal Commission on Government Organization* (Regina, 1965), 288.
25 / Interview with Mr G. Powers, Deputy Minister, Newfoundland Department of Supply.
26 / Interview with Mr R. Borrowman, Director of Purchases, Saskatchewan Purchasing Agency.
27 / MacDonald interview.
28 / E.g., 50 per cent in Alberta. Wall interview.
29 / See *Saskatchewan Royal Commission on Government Organization.*
30 / Alberta Queen's Printer, Budget Expenditure Study ms., 1964.
31 / MacDonald interview.
32 / Peterson interview.
33 / O'Brien interview.
34 / Confidential source.
35 / Interview with Mr L.S.M. Partridge, Assistant Deputy Minister, Treasury Department, Manitoba.
36 / Quebec does not qualify because distribution of free publications is still highly decentralized.
37 / Hon. C. S. MacNaughton, "Statement on Common Services," 2 November 1967.
38 / Interview with Mr S. Smith, Advisory Services Division, Ontario Treasury Board.

4
Publication distribution: government systems

Extreme administrative decentralization entangles the distribution of provincial publications as much as it confuses the processes of production. In fact, the problems associated with it are intensified. In addition, distribution is endowed with many problems of its own; particularly problems of the criteria used to select documents eligible for distribution, out-of-print materials, selection of depositories, and the structure and use of mailing lists.

DISTRIBUTION STRUCTURES

Most governments devolve distribution responsibility upon their member agencies and in many instances, these in turn require their subordinate units to handle the documents most relevant to their particular activities.[1] As in the case of document production, the departments publishing the greatest number of items tended to exhibit the most sophisticated procedures for handling them. Departments of agriculture and departments created to promote provincial economic growth, for example, have developed mass mailing facilities, check-lists, reciprocal distribution arrangements, and even cataloguing procedures. Departments having little or no cause to communicate with the general public, and consequently publishing rarely, possess virtually no techniques for distributing the few items they do produce. Although no fixed procedures exist in any of the provinces, the following generalizations can be made.

Atlantic Provinces

In the Atlantic provinces, production of all types of documents is extremely limited and distribution is carried out either at the departmental or divisional level. The more active publishing departments attempt to maintain mailing lists, but assign them to lower-level personnel, who are not trained to discriminate

DISTRIBUTION: GOVERNMENT SYSTEMS / 35

between receivers of documents and tend to prune lists without warning. In only one department studied, the Newfoundland Department of Natural Resources, was the mailing list reviewed by higher-level personnel. In addition, none of the departments interviewed appear to have adopted the practice of warning recipients that their "subscription" might be cancelled. It must be remembered, however, that although the departments interviewed tended to be the most active in the publishing field, they were far from a majority of the governmental agencies in each province.

Departments maintaining mailing lists appear to be very few in number. For the most part, documents are mailed out in response to specific requests. As few departments assign responsibility for distribution to any one office, this chore is usually handled by the secretarial staff of the branch responsible for the document. Frequently, requests receive a low priority or are allowed to pile up until a sufficient number have accumulated to make the job seem "worthwhile" to the clerk. The result is inconvenience to the client and poor public relations for the government.

As chapter 3 suggests, the regions' Queen's Printers can seldom provide documents requested of them by the public. The fact that the federal Queen's Printer is a distributor of documents misleads many members of the public, including librarians and academics, into believing that the provincial Queen's Printers have the same function. Only the Nova Scotian Queen's Printer distributes more than a very limited number of publications and he does not offer many more than those available from his regional counterparts. The distribution responsibilities usually assigned the Queen's Printer cover only the statutes and *Gazette*. From time to time, too, the Queen's Printers of Prince Edward Island, Nova Scotia, and New Brunswick may distribute documents having no easily identifiable home (most frequently royal commission reports).

However, while they cannot themselves supply requested documents, they frequently go to considerable lengths to assist enquirers. Even in Newfoundland, where the Queen's Printer is actually a commercial printer, efforts are made through the Department of Supply to ensure that requests reach the appropriate department. The New Brunswick and Nova Scotian Queen's Printers provide the same assistance. In Prince Edward Island, the Queen's Printer forwards requests to the Legislative Librarian, Mr Douglas Boylan, who has compiled the following form-letter reply:

I have received your recent inquiry concerning publications of the Government of Prince Edward Island. Though we have attempted to establish a central distribution office our efforts, to the present, have not been successful. The Legislative Library and the Queen's Printer do not distribute publications: we have only deposit copies.

The following information may be of some assistance to you:
  1 Departmental publications are distributed by the issuing authority.

Requests are best addressed to the office of the Deputy Minister of the Department concerned.

2 An up-to-date list of departments, boards, and commissions is printed annually in the *Canadian Almanac and Directory*.

3 Publications of the Legislative Assembly are distributed by the Clerk of the Assembly.

4 In most cases, publications are distributed free of charge. Printing runs are often small, and titles are often soon out-of-print.

5 A request for a standing order cannot be relied upon: an annual request is much more effective.

6 Most publications are printed early in the year, in anticipation of tabling in the Legislative Assembly. I would suggest that the best time to request material would be in February or March.

7 Neither a catalogue of publications nor a telephone directory is published.

Again I regret that we are unable to help you directly but I hope that my comments may be of some assistance to you.

Most of this advice could be duplicated for all the provinces save Quebec and, to an extent, Ontario.

The Queen's Printers are not the only agencies providing an informal finding service. Legislative libraries, despite being badly understaffed, have often done this.

In an attempt to diminish their burden, Table 4:1 has been prepared to outline the agencies usually responsible for distributing the various types of documents published by the governments of this region. If used in conjunction with Mr Boylan's advice and the data presented in chapter 6 this information should overcome a few of the problems of acquiring Atlantic provinces documents. Tables 4:2 and 4:3 present similar data for the western and central provinces.

The Newfoundland government has occasionally innovated its distribution procedures. On several occasions, it has arranged for the sale of documents through local booksellers, but officials report that there have been few sales and that usually almost all stock is returned to the government. Despite this lack of success, the government determined to use the same technique to obtain the widest possible circulation for the report of the recent royal commission on education and, apparently, better results were achieved. The Newfoundland government also reported the only attempt by a province to distribute materials through the federal Queen's Printer. The item concerned - *The Fighting Newfoundlander* - was a history of the Royal Newfoundland Regiment and the results of the experiment will disappoint those who have urged co-operative arrangements between the provincial governments and the federal agency; the Newfoundland government felt that little was done to properly advertise the book and the arrangement has been terminated.[2]

TABLE 4:1

Distributors of selected categories of Atlantic provinces publications

Type of document	Distributing agent:			
	Newfoundland	Prince Edward Island	Nova Scotia	New Brunswick
Debates: Leg. Assembly	Budget speech, estimates, distributed by Dept. of Supply	Budget speech, throne speech: clerk of the Assembly, Provincial Secretary; major statements for press from minister concerned	Mr J. Stuewe ed. of Debates, Province House Halifax (mailing list for session only)	Clerk of the Assembly
Sessional documents: Leg. Assembly	Clerk of Assembly	Clerk of Assembly	Queen's Printer	Clerk of the Assembly
Provincial statutes	Queen's Printer	Provincial Secretary	Queen's Printer	Queen's Printer
Regulations	Depts.	Depts.	Dept. or Queen's Printer	Queen's Printer
Dept. Annual Reports	Depts.	Depts.	Dept. or Queen's Printer	Depts.
Dept. publications	Depts.	Depts.	Depts. or Queen's Printer	Depts.
Publications for which fee charged	Depts.	Depts.	Depts. or Queen's Printer	Depts.
Royal Commission Reports/studies	Depts., Dept. of Supply[a], Dept. of Provincial Affairs	n/a	Queen's Printer	Queen's Printer
Public accounts	Dept. of Finance or Supply[a]	Provincial Treasurer	Queen's Printer	Provincial Printer
Gazette	Queen's Printer	Queen's Printer	Queen's Printer	Queen's Printer

[a]While Department of Supply handles publications, approval for distribution has to come from department concerned.

Two other features of the situation in the Atlantic provinces are worthy of note. As has been suggested, the Newfoundland Department of Supply has functions comparable to those of the Queen's Printers in the other provinces; this includes storing and distributing documents such as the *Public Accounts*. However, while the department has the responsibility for the physical handling of these items, mailing lists are determined by the departments supervising publication, and acquisition requests have to be directed to the responsible department.

In Nova Scotia, the Queen's Printer, who distributes a slightly wider range of documents than most of his counterparts, inserts in each serial publication a short form by which the receiver can ask to be placed on the next year's mailing list. This removes the burden of maintaining the mailing list from the Queen's Printer's staff, probably effecting some savings. However, libraries find it difficult to adapt their procedures to this system; the fact that Nova Scotia is the only province following this practice creates problems, which are exacerbated by the high staff turnover in many libraries. A further difficulty stems from the fact that Nova Scotian documents handled by the departments rather than the Queen's Printer are not processed in this way. It is probable that some slight amendments to the procedure - for example, a special mailing list status for certain kinds of institutions - could correct these deficiencies. At the moment, technical difficulties in a basically workable system have created such confusion that Nova Scotia's reputation in this field is unnecessarily low.

Western Provinces

Practice in the Prairie provinces and British Columbia is very similar to that in the Atlantic region. Responsibility for distribution is diffused; Queen's Printers distribute certain statutory documents and those that cannot readily be assigned to any other agency but all other items are the responsibility of the issuing department. Differences occur in administrative detail; western departments reported frequently that they maintain mailing lists and that they notify subscribers before dropping their names from the lists. Also they are more likely than their Atlantic counterparts to produce a wide range of documents with longer print runs.

The Alberta government has introduced a few measures not generally followed in the provinces. The chief of these is the creation of the Alberta Publicity Bureau, a division of the Department of Industry. In addition to distributing its own Department's publications, it will distribute for other departments on request. From time to time, the Bureau has advertised Alberta publications in newspapers, a rare procedure in provincial publishing; usually departments advertise through press releases, their own check-lists, and annual reports, and through displays at exhibitions. The Publicity Bureau's promotion of the newsletter *Within our Borders* in the spring of 1968 entailed placing an

TABLE 4:2

Distributors of selected categories of western provinces publications

Type of document	Distributing agent			
	Manitoba	Saskatchewan	Alberta	British Columbia
Debates: Leg. Assembly	Queen's Printer	Clerk of Leg.	Clerk of Leg. Assembly[a]	
Sessional documents: Leg. Assembly	Queen's Printer/ Clerk of Leg.	Queen's Printer/ Clerk of Leg.	Clerk of Leg. Assembly	Queen's Printer
Provincial statutes	Queen's Printer	Queen's Printer	Queen's Printer	Queen's Printer
Regulations	Depts.	Depts.	Depts.	Depts.
Dept. annual reports	Depts.	Depts.	Depts.	Depts.
Dept. publications	Depts.	Depts.	Dept./Publicity Bureau of Dept. of Industry & Development	Depts.
Publications for which fee charged	Depts.	Depts./Queen's Printer	Dept./Queen's Printer	Depts.
Royal Commission Reports/studies	Queen's Printer	Queen's Printer	Queen's Printer	Queen's Printer/ Provincial Secretary
Public Accounts	Provincial Treasurer	Provincial Treasurer	Provincial Treasurer	Provincial Treasurer
Gazette	Queen's Printer	Queen's Printer	Queen's Printer	Queen's Printer

[a] Alberta does not publish a "Hansard," but photocopies of the official transcript have recently been made available at a cost of 5c per page. The 1968 transcript covered 4,000 pages.

TABLE 4:3

Distributors of selected categories of Ontario and Quebec publications

Type of document	Distributing agent	
	Quebec	Ontario
Debates: Leg. Assembly	Accountant of the Leg. Assembly	Clerk of the Legislature
Sessional documents: Leg. Assembly	Accountant of the Leg. Assembly	Clerk of the Legislature/ Queen's Printer and Publisher[b]
Provincial statutes	Quebec Official Publisher	Queen's Printer
Regulations	Depts./Quebec Official Publisher	Depts.[a]/Queen's Printer and Publisher[b]
Dept. annual reports	Depts./Quebec Official Publisher	Depts.[a]/Queen's Printer and Publisher[b]
Dept. publications	Depts./Quebec Official Publisher	Depts.[a]/Queen's Printer and Publisher[b]
Publications for which fee charged	Depts./Quebec Official Publisher	Depts.[a]/Queen's Printer and Publisher[b]
Royal Commission Reports/studies	Quebec Official Publisher	Dept. or agency concerned/ Queen's Printer and Publisher[b]
Public accounts	Quebec Official Publisher	Provincial Treasurer/Queen's Printer and Publisher[b]
Gazette	Quebec Official Publisher	Queen's Printer and Publisher

[a]Many Ontario departments possess departmental libraries staffed by professional librarians who will frequently provide needed assistance acquiring departmental publications.

[b]The Ontario Queen's Printer and Publisher does not carry all the materials published by the various departments and agencies.

advertisement in every weekly and daily in the Province at a cost of $4,000. The campaign drew requests for 3,000 new subscriptions. The use of private booksellers to distribute the Alberta Government's *White Paper on Human Resources* was also noted, but details on the frequency of use and the success of this technique were not available.

Quebec

The Quebec Queen's Printer (now the Quebec Official Publisher) was established in 1869 with responsibility, like his counterparts in the other provinces, for printing and distributing the *Quebec Official Gazette* and the *Statutes*. In 1960, with the general reorganization of the bureau, the Printer assumed responsibility for distributing a wider range of publications. Starting modestly, the bureau handled only two documents, the *Report* of the Royal Commission of Inquiry on Constitutional Problems (Tremblay Commission) and the *Public Accounts*, through direct and mail-order sales. By 1964, a dozen titles were offered, and at the end of that year, eighty; by March 1967, four hundred publications were being sold through a new Quebec City bookstore and through the mails. In the fiscal year, 1966-7 revenue from the sale of Quebec government publications amounted to $130,164, excluding revenue from documents sold by individual departments.

Many librarians have cited Quebec's Official Publisher as a model for other provinces to imitate. Unfortunately, Quebec's structure, while an improvement on that of all the other provinces, is still far from adequate. The central difficulty, apart from too infrequent production of a list of publications, stems from the fact that many libraries wish to obtain a much wider range of documents than the publisher distributes. They find that the distribution service excludes limited-run processed documents and free items available from the various departments. They are thus forced to contact the Quebec government Office of Information and Publicity, which centralizes distribution of some free materials, or the departments themselves, most of which have an information director responsible for dealing with such requests. In other words, as far as the major library is concerned, the problems involved in locating and acquiring many Quebec documents are only slightly diminished; the difficult and time-consuming task of maintaining a relationship with each department continues. Even the Quebec National Library, which has the most powerful depository legislation in effect in any province, reports that it has difficulty obtaining all Quebec documents. Those sold are estimated to represent only a quarter of the Quebec documents of interest to the library.

Ontario

Ontario's system of document distribution, with its structure for production, is currently being reorganized. There is, then, little to be gained from an account of the situation that has existed in the province. A few details are provided later in this chapter as a part of a discussion of the need for depository libraries in Ontario. On the other hand, it has not been possible to obtain a satisfactory description of current operating procedures from the Queen's Printer and Publisher, Mr William Kinmond. Hence, the best that can be offered here is a brief outline of the new policy proposed in 1967-8, a brief exploration of some of its implications, and a sketch of the structure now in operation drawn from a press release and the foreword to a document entitled *Ontario Government Publications Catalogue*.

The distributive aspects of the original scheme included:

(a) Appointment of a Queen's Publisher ... [who would] advise [author departments] on printing processes, the number of press runs, sale prices and the avenues to be promoted to achieve the desired degree of social and economic impact,
(b) A central mail-order depot,
(c) Maintenance of an up-to-date catalogue of Ontario publications [about 1,500 in number],
(d) A system of official depositories in university libraries and selected public libraries across the province,
(e) A bookshop for over-the-counter sales of government publications.[3]

It is understood that the Queen's Publisher was to be responsible for recording copyright for Ontario publications and for providing certain bibliographic services to libraries within the province.[4] The Department of Public Works was to operate central duplicating services and central mailing services within the new structure.[5] The underlying philosophy of the proposal was that the Queen's Publisher in his capacity as distributor as well as publisher should convince the departments that he and his organization could provide a service which they would be foolish to ignore. As the main contact for libraries obtaining Ontario publications, he would have an equally exacting task meeting their needs and interpreting them to the publishing departments.

On paper the new system suggested a major improvement over existing practice in the province; its success would depend, however, on the ingenuity and diplomacy of the new official as he attempted to capture the custom of client departments and on the willingness of the government to provide him with the requisite staff.

One possible failing in the original proposal was provided for early in 1970 when the Queen's Printer and Publisher, now located within the Department of Public Works, assumed responsibility for the production of processed documents. The earlier proposal to divide responsibility with the Provincial Secretary suggested that the same difficulties confronting the librarian attempting to obtain Quebec's processed documents would be discovered in Ontario. Whether or not a common administrative home has effected co-ordination of effort remains to be seen, however. The location of that home within the Department of Public Works, a department which has had little experience with publishing, as opposed to printing, does not suggest that the library community and the public in general will find the service entirely satisfactory.

An indication of the lack of contact between the new organization and the library community is to be found in the *Ontario Government Publications Catalogue,* which is briefly described in chapter 6 and which reflects considerable inexperience in the compilation of finding aids of this sort.

There is little else by which to judge the new organization. A bookstore was opened near the Ontario Government Buildings and certainly offers a service that is an improvement over that which had previously existed. But the store does not carry all the official publications of the various publishing departments, a deficiency which will perpetuate many of the frustrations traditionally encountered by those seeking to acquire provincial government publications. A press release issued by the agency reports that the "Queen's Printer and Publisher is now also supplying services required by departments in preparation of their publications" and that the office "organized the printing and distribution of the Guide to Ontario Government Services and is responsible for keeping this publication up-to-date." Further information concerning these services - other than the evidence offered by the documents themselves - was not available; nor was it possible to discover whether the new agency proposes to offer any of the bibliographic services suggested in the original proposal.

A depository system is envisaged, however. The introduction to the publications catalogue contains the following information:

The Queen's Publisher shall distribute without charge one copy of any government publication classified as not being for internal use only to designated libraries in Ontario for preservation so that the public may have access to all government publications.

Full Depositories
Full Depository Libraries automatically receive one copy of the government publications free of charge.

Selective Depositories
The Queen's Publisher shall provide free of charge one copy of each publication listed in the monthly check-lists to selective depositories provided selections are made from the monthly check-lists within 30 days of its issue.

We have been unable to discover whether designation has yet taken place or what procedures have been established to effect designation or to classify documents. At mid-summer 1970 no monthly check-lists had appeared.

MAILING LISTS

Departmental use of mailing lists as an aid to distribution has been referred to from time to time in the preceding description of distribution practices. Since the mailing list itself influences the distribution pattern of a publication, it deserves further discussion.

Mailing lists vary considerably in scope and sophistication, more from department to department than from government to government. Almost invariably, departments of trade and industry possess highly developed lists; equally, departments of attorneys-general do not. The mailing list is a major communications tool for the one, a peripheral luxury for the other. The librarian finds the acquisition of documents affected accordingly.

Generally, departments can be grouped into three categories in so far as their use of mailing lists is concerned. The first group publishes few documents and does not maintain any list at all. The second maintains a simple one, which is amended only to the extent that new names are added and others are deleted when publications are returned by the Post Office. Usually, the department will create a separate list for each publication it issues on a regular basis. The third approach utilizes a single list for the entire range of documents issued by the department, but breaks the list down into categories of recipients so that combinations of segments can be strung together to create a mailing list suitable for each type of document distributed. A typical list of this sort, built up by a department of trade and industry consists of five groups, each group representing a sector of the community considered significant. Provincial manufacturers are represented in one group, municipal agencies and officials in another, and so on. Each group is in turn divided into between five and thirteen subgroups with each subgroup coded separately to facilitate breakdown and creation of lists for specific purposes. Responsibility for maintaining the list, which in May 1968 included over twenty thousand names, is divided between six officials each of whom services those subgroups that are most closely related to his main departmental responsibility. Names are added in part on request, but more frequently as a result of departmental research.

Such minor details of a mundane aspect of the distribution process can profoundly affect library acquisitions. For example, the department that does not maintain a mailing list may still occasionally prepare documents for distribution. Because it does not generally publish, and very likely would not issue a check-list, the department's publication is likely to be overlooked by the librarian unless, through the diligence of the legislative library, it should be added to that collection and thence find its way into *Canadiana*.

Again, the calibre of the staff handling mailing lists may affect the library's chances of receiving departmental publications. Many libraries complain that they are dropped from mailing lists without warning and they attribute this to the fact that the lists are usually maintained by low-echelon staff who become careless or lazy. In defence of such staff, officials responsible for maintaining mailing lists, point out that libraries frequently fail to return revision notices.* Employee calibre can affect distribution in another respect. Many libraries ask to be added to all departmental mailing lists. A clerk receiving such a request and not fully understanding the library's needs may use his own discretion to decide which publications the library is really anxious to obtain. This exercise of discretion may also explain why libraries sometimes cease receiving publications; a clerk revising a mailing list has decided that the library "is not really interested" in certain publications. Libraries attempt to meet this problem by specifying precisely what publications they want, by trying to explain their needs, or, in one case,[6] by writing a periodic "thank-you" letter to the agency involved.

The most sophisticated lists are frequently the most difficult for the library to contend with. The careful categorization of names not only helps determine who should receive publications; it also suggests who should not. The library's receipt of a publication will often depend on the general category to which the subgroup university libraries is accorded. In the list cited earlier, the university libraries' subgroup appears under the general grouping of "Press." Unless the official servicing this group is acutely aware of library needs, it is possible that libraries on this list receive only the more bland, propagandistic offerings of the department. Similarly, research libraries will note the ominous exclusion of a subgrouping entitled "research libraries." Such an exclusion suggests that all libraries are treated alike, more probably to the disadvantage of libraries building a very complete collection than to the advantage of those that are not. Again, a very great deal depends on the official servicing the group and the success the library has had in educating him to its needs.

Dissatisfaction with the mailing procedures used by departments has been expressed by treasury officials in several provinces. One, questioning their usefulness, commented that "some departments are very vague about who is using their publications."[7] Another province investigated its mass mailing facilities and discovered that:

Seventeen of the departments now have 55 pieces of addressing equipment, 37 printers and 18 platemakers. In all, there is an inventory of some 400,000 plates which are used to make 5.5 million impressions each year - A staff of seventeen is employed in these addressing operations.

A survey of the address plates indicated that there is probably considerable duplication. Most departments have separate mailing lists of:

T.V. and Radio Stations
Newspapers

*These are postcards circulated by the publishing agency bearing the name and address of the subscriber and asking return of the card to ensure continuation of the subscription.

Members of the Legislature
   Municipal Officials
   Schools, Educational Institutions
   Libraries

No co-ordination exists between departments; consequently, the addressing equipment is under-utilized.[8]

Such studies are leading, and have led, to a greater degree of centralization of mass mailing facilities. Usually, the facility itself is centralized while the departments preserve their control over the actual composition of the lists. However, it is highly likely that provincial lists will gradually be created, subdivisions of which could be pulled together to form various combinations to achieve a wide range of different purposes. The introduction of centralization in this field can be of great help to libraries or it can severely damage acquisition programs. If libraries are treated as a single subgroup of a general "press" group, it is highly probable that they will not receive the materials they desire. However, if libraries are given a separate category of their own and if the mailing procedures for that category are carefully related to an adequate depository system, it is possible that many of the problems that currently plague the librarian would be eliminated. This cannot be achieved without effort. If libraries wish to take advantage of such centralization, they must persuade governments that theirs is a valid, logical, and desirable request.

PERPETUATION OF DECENTRALIZED SYSTEMS OF DISTRIBUTION

Although librarians, academics, and members of the general public anxious to obtain elusive information seldom have a kind word to say for current distribution systems, many administrators maintain that this system is the most effective method of putting information in the hands it can best serve. Departments argue that they are best qualified to advise the public on matters related to their own jurisdiction. They point out that under a centralized system, the Queen's Printer, or some other central agency, would meet requests for information with reading suggestions that might not be helpful. Such an agent could not be expected to be familiar with every matter administered by the government of which he is a part. Departments, however, by direct contact with enquirers, can not only supply the most appropriate literature, but can offer supplementary informal advice on the enquirer's specific problem.

At least two Queen's Printers disagreed with this assessment, arguing that many members of the public ask for specific publications and are disgruntled at having to traipse from department to department collecting separate official statements on a single problem. The Queen's Printer of New Brunswick counters the "specialized knowledge" argument with a similar view of his own, pointing out that there are times when his knowledge can assist departments. He cites one case in which a department ordered twenty-five extra subscriptions to the *Royal Gazette* so that field personnel would be able to keep abreast of changes in regulations. The Queen's Printer pointed out that the field staff would soon tire of checking the closely printed notices of the *Gazette* for occasional changes in regulations. He suggested, instead, that the department receive extra page proofs of the regulations it had to publish in the *Gazette.* This solution proved acceptable.[9] In Quebec the individual who needs more information than is provided in publications contacts the relevant department directly. There he can be supplied with specialized information or with publications more relevant to his needs than those he has chosen from the catalogue of the Quebec Official Publisher. Furthermore, the possibility that a central distributor will not know what publications would best meet individual needs is offset by other factors. In particular, it is unlikely that an individual who has taken the trouble to study a subject will long be satisfied with irrelevant material or, if he feels it necessary, will delay contacting the agency directly. It is more likely that centralization, rather than discouraging interest, will foster it. The person who has not contacted a department, because he does not know that it can help him or does not know where to apply, may find the Queen's Publisher's bookstore or catalogue an important introduction to a host of new information sources.

Obviously, there are arguments in favour of both points of view and a compromise of some sort should be possible. Some alternative solutions will be discussed in a later chapter.

The continuation of a system of decentralized distribution is also explained by theories such as: "civil servants like to be identified with the fruits of their labour - so, they like to control distribution," or "departments do not like to lose parts of their empires." Hence, many librarians associated with governments, treasury department officials, and Queen's Printers' staff believe that a move toward centralization would be fiercely opposed by the departments. This is not necessarily true. While some departmental officials expressed antagonism to the idea, others did not, referring to distribution activities as a chore that could be handled by a central body if arrangements could be made for the department to retain direct contact with members of the public. Thus, the "ag. rep." must still be in a position to supply farmers with needed information, regardless of the fact that the farmers can obtain publications from a central office, and the department of industry must still be primarily responsible for contacting potential investors.

An even more powerful factor, however, is the department's realization that "documents ... are instruments of policy" and that their control helps determine the ability of the department to manipulate itself and its policies independently of central authority. One example effectively illustrates this process. "We have run into trouble because the Budget Speech and the Department of [Industry's] brochures are directly contradictory. It is the Department of Industry's job to be optimistic and the Budget Speech must be conservative. The Treasurer is concerned about our credit reputation, so he has to make realistic estimates of what will happen."

Again, centralization itself, as we have suggested in chapter 3, is not always considered to be the necessarily obvious solution. Too many central agencies have failed to live up to the expectations held for them; too often operating departments have had to devise schemes to avoid central services. Today, a central service has to prove itself by providing a real service and not many senior decision-makers will accept a proposal for centralization unless it can be clearly demonstrated that existing services are totally unsatisfactory and that the proposed operation will be able to perform much more effectively than the agencies it replaces.

There are two other factors tending to perpetuate the present system. The first is the question of cost; many senior administrators genuinely believe that central distribution is too costly for their provinces. They may well be right. For example, they point out that central distribution requires extensive warehouse facilities.[10] Where today back issues of departmental publications are stored in any convenient cubbyhole, central distribution would require warehouse space and elaborate techniques for inventory control. Similarly, clerical workers who now carry out distribution activities as a minor part of their duties could not be fired or brought into the new structure. They would continue their former jobs and new employees would be hired to handle the new operation.

The second is a combination of perplexity and inertia. On the one hand, it is only relatively recently that pressure has been applied to governments to improve distribution procedures. Even where changes are being introduced, surprisingly few demand inputs have brought them about. Seeing no cause to change, governments have not changed, preferring to expend their energies where innovations have been demanded. Again, many government officials express willingness to help, but as one asked, "how do you deal with so many different kinds of distribution?"[11] To an extent, as we have suggested, those agencies that have introduced new policies have done so at the risk of ignoring some of the more unmanageable problems involved, notably the problems of supplying processed and free documents to libraries and genuinely interested members of the public. This inertia and perplexity includes not only the distributing departments and the central treasury officials, but also, from time to time, the Queen's Printers themselves who fear having to assume responsibilities of unknown proportions with but limited resources of staff and money.

NOTES

1 / Data obtained from interviews and responses to questionnaires.
2 / Interview with Mr J.G. Channing, Deputy Minister of the Department of Provincial Affairs.

3 / Letter from Mr J.S. Yoerger, Deputy Provincial Secretary to A. Pross, 13 May 1968.
4 / Interview with Mr S. Smith, Advisory Services Division, Ontario Treasury Board.
5 / Letter from the Hon. Ray Connell to A.P. Pross, 16 May 1968.
6 / Simon Fraser University Library.
7 / Interview with Mr A.D. O'Brien, Provincial Treasurer's Department, Alberta.
8 / Confidential source.
9 / Interview with Mr W.A. Peterson.
10 / Interview with Mr A. Wells, Executive Assistant to Premier Campbell of Prince Edward Island. Supported by interviews with several Queen's Printers.
11 / Interview with Mr B.M. Hudson, Queen's Printer's Office, Manitoba.

5
Output to input: the difficult task of acquiring provincial government publications

Our discussion so far has concentrated on the distribution structure as it has evolved within the various agencies of the provincial governments. Little has been said to indicate how the system affects the individual librarian and members of the public. The following paragraphs are intended to give only a brief impression of the difficulties that occur. Reference is made to specific illustrations of these difficulties and in chapter 6 a lengthy discussion of search and acquisition techniques describes the chores that are created and the costs that are incurred by the chaotic nature of the provincial distribution structure.

One crucially important factor that will be dealt with in chapter 6, rather than here, is the lack of adequate check-lists and bibliographies to supply the librarian or the researcher with a suitable starting point. Searching for a needle in a haystack is frustrating; not knowing whether the needle exists is devastating.

Decentralization presents difficulties because of the wide variation in procedures that inevitably occurs. The librarian attempting to build a good provincial documents collection must create an individual relationship with each agency of every government and frequently with the various subdivisions of each agency. Even the legislative librarian finds this a daunting task, which, for all the effort it involves, frequently fails to achieve the desired results. The plight of the scholar or librarian who is far removed from the government concerned is easy to imagine. However, decentralization does not necessarily involve departmental unwillingness to help the library or the general public. Most academics, for example, reported that, although attempts to obtain publications usually involved writing more than one letter to more than one possible source, replies to enquiries were always prompt and courteous. In the interviews conducted during this survey, only one official expressed unwillingness to meet library requests, arguing that although libraries are sent "whatever they ask for within reason, keeping librarians well informed is not the chief function of the Bureau."[1] In general, librarians agree that once the existence of a document is known, it is not too difficult to obtain, and usually, departmental officials are extremely helpful. What does hamper the librarian is the fact that it is hard to discover a document's existence and time-consuming to obtain it. In illustrating the last point, one librarian reported waiting two months to receive an Alberta government document that had been advertised in the newspapers.[2]

Despite the helpfulness of government officials, librarians frequently find that they are of little real assistance, that they too are handicapped by the fact that they do not always know what has been published by their own department, where it is available, or whether the item can be released to the public. One member of a Department of Industry and Commerce complained, "our department does not know what other departments in the same government are putting out. Also, we often have to request a publication several times before it comes."

DEPOSITORY LIBRARIES

Government documents librarians, contrasting the difficulties of acquiring provincial publications with the relative ease with which depository libraries obtain United States, Canadian, and United Nations documents, frequently suggest the introduction of a similar system at the provincial level. Unfortunately, a depository system is only as efficient as the distribution system upon which it depends. The experience of those libraries that have been designated provincial depositories indicates that as long as the production and distribution of documents is highly decentralized, designation is relatively meaningless. The underlying problem of decentralization finds expression in three problems encountered where deposition has been officially recognized:

1 Legislation creating depositories cannot be enforced. It simply provides the librarian with a measure of authority to support a demand.

2 As long as there is no reliable guide to the production of publications, depositories are unable to determine what publications they should have and thus are unable to insist on deposition.

3 Depository legislation does not define the type of document that must be deposited. Hence, much material never finds its way into deposit collections, unless auxiliary acquisition procedures are introduced.

A fourth problem has emerged in those jurisdictions where the legislative library acts as collector and distributor. This is simply the problem that the library is given too little manpower and financial assistance to carry out the task effectively.

These problems are illustrated by examination of those depository systems in effect in the provinces. Of the fifty-three libraries (other than the Library of Parliament and the National Library) for which data are available, twenty-one, representing all but one of the provinces, reported themselves to be depositories for publications of their own province. These are listed in Table 5:1.

TABLE 5:1

*Provincial libraries reporting and/or
accorded depository status for provincial government publications*[3]

Library	1 Libraries reporting themselves depositories	2 Libraries officially designated depositories[a]
Newfoundland Public Archives	X	X
Newfoundland Legislative Library	X	X
Nova Scotia Legislative Library	X	X
St Francis Xavier University Library	X	
New Brunswick Legislative Library	X	X
University of New Brunswick Library	X	X
Quebec Legislative Library	X	X
Quebec National Library	X	X
Laval University Library		X
University of Sherbrooke Library		X
Bishop's University Library		X
Bibliothèque de l'Ecole des Hautes Etudes Commerciales		X
McGill University Library	X	X
Sir George Williams University Library	X	X
University of Montreal Library	X	X
Laurentian University Library	X	
Ontario Archives	X (partial)	
Provincial Library of Manitoba	X	X
University of Manitoba Library	X (partial)	X
Saskatchewan Archives	X	
Saskatchewan Legislative Library	X	
Alberta Provincial Library	X	X
British Columbia Provincial Library	X	X
Simon Fraser University Library	X	
University of British Columbia Library	X	X

[a]See Appendix II for terms of legislative authorization of depository status.

The statistic is, however, of little value and in some cases can be interpreted to mean only that these libraries are receiving some provincial publications, something that can be said of the majority of libraries in the country. This is because the term "depository" has several meanings. For a few libraries listed above, it means nothing more than the fact that the library is on the mailing lists of several government departments. More frequently it indicates that the library receives on a fairly regular basis the statutory publications of the government. Some libraries appear to consider themselves depositories even though most acquisitions have to be searched for and ordered individually. In a few cases, the library has been officially designated a depository by the government concerned.

If we re-examine the list to exclude all libraries that do not receive automatically three-quarters of the statutory publications of their home province, we eliminate some of the smaller university libraries. If we exclude all but those libraries that have been officially designated depositories, the list includes only the libraries checked in column 2 of Table 5:1.

A far more rigorous elimination would occur if we excluded those libraries that do not automatically receive 50 per cent or more of the processed documents prepared for limited but public distribution by departments. This, however, is impossible, there being no accurate appraisals of the quantity of material of this sort that is prepared. On the basis of the data collected during the survey, this would mean that no library in Canada could claim depository status.

How then should a "depository library" be described? The mere receipt of provincial publications is too broad a definition; almost any Canadian library could qualify for this status. Is official designation the operative criterion? Designation is certainly essential, since deposition is a privilege that entails obligations and consequently some authoritative body has to accord the privilege and ensure that the obligations are being duly observed. But in the Canadian provincial context, designation, as we shall show, has proven insufficient. Further ingredients have to be added: notably (1) that a depository library should be entitled to receive documents automatically and (2) the range of documents eligible for deposit has to be broad enough to include limited-edition public processed documents as well as statutory documents. In other words, a depository library can be defined as a library designated as a depository by the relevant publishing government and, consequently, entitled to receive automatically all publications, pamphlets, or circulars issued or released by a department or agency of the government for general or limited public distribution.[4] Were this definition to be applied to the list of libraries claiming depository status only the Legislative Library of Nova Scotia would emerge as having, on paper, undisputed right to the designation. In all other instances, the legislative authority includes a restrictive clause such as that of New Brunswick's, which orders the Queen's Printer "to distribute to the Legislative Library ... four copies of whatever is printed under [the Queen's Printer] Act";[5] or that of Manitoba, which refers to "every official publication in any form of printing or processing" but confines deposition to those "available for public information in numbers for general distribution."[6] The pre-eminence of the Legislative Library of Nova Scotia exists on paper only, for, while it is entitled to receive the various publications automatically, no effective machinery exists to accomplish automatic deposit, and Miss Shirley Elliott, Legislative Librarian, reports that acquisition is often ensured only by checking with each individual department.

It may be argued that this definition is unnecessarily rigorous, that the standard of service provided by most of the libraries considering themselves depositories is adequate. In response, perhaps we need only point out, first, that researchers have commented extremely critically on the quality of the documents most frequently deposited under existing systems. As one academic commented "none of the libraries I use (University of Alberta, Alberta Provincial Library, or government department libraries) has an extensive or intensive end in mind. I always have doubts about their completeness." Secondly, that government officials have themselves not only agreed with researchers but have commented that the likeliest sources of useful information are processed documents prepared in limited quantity but far more frequently than statutory or tabled materials. On these grounds alone, current definitions of depository status need to be revised.

The introduction of a rigorous definition is not intended to disparage the work of existing depository libraries. They and their counterparts not officially recognized as depositories have done a great deal to ensure the preservation of adequate collections of documents. Their problem is that under existing conditions, they cannot perform this function without a great deal of unnecessary expenditure of time and money and they can never be sure that they have achieved their goal. An appreciation of these problems follows from examination of the depository arrangements currently in effect.

The most fortunate libraries are those designated depositories by their respective governments. Official authority may not ensure automatic deposit; it does bear an authority that government departments and agencies understand and observe. Of these, the British Columbia Provincial Library may be the most successful in obtaining the documents needed for its collection. This measure of success can be attributed to the fact that the library is able to obtain documents from a production source that is the most highly centralized of all the provinces.* The system is reported to work well, although the University of British Columbia Library noted that its status had "threatened to lapse" early in 1968 and that some of the more costly items are sometimes not included.[7] Where processed documents are concerned, however, the British Columbia depository libraries are in much the same position as libraries in other provinces. Depository status confers some authority - even when it does not strictly apply - but time must still be spent discovering what documents exist and then persuading departments and agencies to provide copies.

In Alberta, the Provincial Library and, in Newfoundland, the Legislative Library both report that they have been designated official depositories, but neither library provided documentation outlining the status accorded by designation. Both reported that they do not "automatically receive all Provincial Government publications," although in Alberta, "most departments see that we

---

*The arrangement with the Queen's Printer is straightforward. The Printer simply keeps three cartons at the end of his production line; as print orders are carried out copies are put in each carton; full cartons are sent to the Provincial Library, the Simon Fraser Library, and the University of British Columbia Library. This procedure ensures that the libraries receive extraneous materials, but does provide all the documents the Queen's Printer handles.

receive publications." In that province "a reminder to departments is sufficient," but in Newfoundland repeated telephone calls and visits are sometimes necessary. The Newfoundland Library estimated that, in time, it is able to acquire all its province's publications, whilst the Alberta Provincial Library claimed 85 per cent success. Both estimates are subject to the qualification that no accurate production figures are available. The Newfoundland Provincial Archives considers itself a depository for published documents only. Its authorizing directive refers to "all reports, pamphlets, newsletters, maps, drawings and other publications of any kind whatsoever which may be prepared for public use ... ." The Provincial Archivist reports that this covers primarily tabled documents although occasionally government documents may be deposited at the archives on a restricted basis. In addition, the Archives receive the copies of every document sent to the Premier's Department, the Department of Provincial Affairs - an arrangement which assures that the collection will include at least the more significant processed documents.[8] Finally, since it is an archival collection, this depository is assured, for as long as its records deposit system is effective, of eventually acquiring a nearly completed collection of processed documents.

The New Brunswick Legislative Library's depository status resulted from a request by the National Library of Canada for copies of all of that province's government publications for inclusion in *Canadiana*.[9] To accomodate this request, an order in council was passed directing the Queen's Printer to send three copies of whatever is printed under the Queen's Printer Act to the Legislative Library.[10] Gradually, the scope of the order was widened so that the Legislative Library now receives twenty copies and distributes them to the Library of Parliament, the Library of Congress, each of the provincial legislative libraries, and each of New Brunswick's university libraries, in addition to the original recipients.[11]

A similar procedure is followed by the Manitoba Provincial Library, which also acquired depository status in 1952. Documents are sent to libraries able to reciprocate by supplying the Provincial Library with the publications of the institutions or agencies to which they are attached. This is the most extensive deposit system operating in the provinces, supplying key governmental and research libraries in the country. Because of the large number of libraries served, the range of documents supplied has to be restricted to annual reports of forty-one government departments and agencies. Three national libraries - the National Library of Canada, the Library of Congress, and the British Museum - also receive copies of all other materials obtained by the Provincial Library. The entire distributive aspect of the operation is handled by one clerical employee and other members of the staff contribute further man-hours by searching out and acquiring items that have not been deposited. In this respect, the library faces the same difficulties as every other depository: "although we have an Order in Council giving us depository status, we have to keep reminding people of it."[12] Depository status, it has been found, can be made effective only if it is supplemented by strong informal liaisons with departments.

In 1967, the Quebec Provincial Secretary's Department announced that "pour raisons d'intérêt public, l'Imprimeur de la reine assurerait, aussitôt que possible, la distribution gratuite et automatique des publications gouvernementales à un certain nombre de bibliothèques, réparties à travers le Québec et ailleurs." The proposed depository status has been accorded Canadian governmental libraries, all Quebec university libraries, and selected public libraries in the province, while additions to the list of legal depositories can be made by the minister. However, although the announcement promised that the designated libraries would be "dépositaires totales," it appears that processed documents and documents distributed free of charge are not covered by the arrangement and libraries building research collections are forced to maintain contacts with individual departments and agencies. Thus, even the Legislative Library and the Quebec National Library do not always receive processed material.

The structure of the Quebec deposit system has proven unsatisfactory to at least one university library. McGill University Library finds that the fact that not all items on deposit are provided free of charge causes delays in acquisition on the library's side, since chargeable items have to be routed through the library's acquisition department, and on the side of the publisher, who seems to need more time to deliver free items. A solution to this problem might involve providing all items for depositories on a free list, or charging depositories a lump sum to cover costs of supplying certain publications.[13]

The experience of governmental libraries that are not designated depositories is not very different from that of those possessing this status. In no province has the legislative library been so successful in educating distributing agencies that it can count on receiving automatically all the documents to which it is entitled. In every province, as is illustrated in chapter 6, elaborate search and acquisition techniques have to be employed. Nevertheless, depository status does lend its possessor a measure of authority and most legislative libraries have established an official or unofficial claim to the title. In Ontario, however, the Legislative Library, in conjunction with the Government Publications Committee of the Ontario Library Association, has sought a more extensive structure than any presently in existence in Canada. Reporting in 1963, the Library Association Committee stated:

There is presently no depository system for Government publications within the Province. While the Legislative Library of Ontario tries to obtain as complete holdings as possible of Ontario Publications, there is no legislation or directive of any kind to support it by requiring that publications be deposited with the Library. The Library is frequently in the position of having to remind agencies of the Government to send copies of their publications to it. Under these circumstances, while the holdings of the Legislative Library are substantial and undoubtedly the best there is, they cannot be called complete.[14]

Pointing out that "such a move would strengthen its hand immeasurably in securing materials from the various agencies of government," the Committee urged that depository status be conferred on the Library and that "a system of regional depositories consisting of certain university and public libraries be set up in the province to ensure the local availability of full sets of publications."[15] The Committee also recognized the significance of processed materials, urging that they, as well as printed documents, be covered by the depository system. Its most significant recommendation was based on the "very effective arrangement" instituted in Louisiana in 1948. There, a depository system is the exclusive responsibility of an official Recorder of Documents who "supplies some 40 official depositories with the publications issued by more than 200 state agencies."[16] In addition to ensuring the fairly prompt delivery of documents to the depositories, the Recorder also issues a monthly check-list, cumulative twice a year. The Committee's recommendation "that a Recorder of Documents be designated and that Ontario government agencies be required to deposit their publications with the Recorder for distribution to depositories," would ensure the creation of a responsibility centre exclusively concerned with tracing and recording Ontario government publications. Such an arrangement would not only institutionalize the procedure of tracing documents, an activity that at present tends to be viewed as but one of the many responsibilities of the legislative library, it would also, by providing the Recorder with a specific area of responsibility, provide a greater incentive than currently exists for the complete recording of documents.

It is difficult to assess the extent of the Committee's influence on the development of the newly created system for the production and distribution of Ontario's government publications. There are conflicting accounts of the origins of the recent policy revision, but the report has been examined in the process of policy revision and some part of its recommendations can be seen reflected in the proposals to award the Queen's Publisher responsibility for filing copyright for government documents and for preparing check-lists and retrospective bibliographies of Ontario's publications, types of activity similar to those proposed for the Recorder of Documents. The decision to recognize various libraries as depositories also reflects the influence of this and other briefs to the Ontario government. However, as we have suggested, the problems involved in obtaining processed documents do not seem to be recognized by the proposed structure. Until an adequate depository system is officially introduced, the situation in Ontario will continue to be the most unsatisfactory in Canada. The Legislative Library's position is slightly improved over that of five years ago; it is now assured of receiving two copies of all documents tabled in the Legislature.[17] But there is no adequate procedure for preparing a check-list of

Ontario documents or of ensuring that documents are listed in *Canadiana,* and all other libraries collecting Ontario materials must spend an inordinate amount of time and money to achieve less than adequate results.

University and public libraries attempting to acquire collections of provincial publications face far greater difficulties than do governmental libraries. Lacking the obvious claim to automatic receipt of publications asserted by the legislative library, several have sought depository status. Thus, Memorial University of Newfoundland has had little difficulty in acquiring annual reports as printed matter but has had great difficulty in acquiring processed material, which one librarian estimates comprises seventy-five per cent of the material needed to build a good research collection of Newfoundland government materials. The library's attempts to acquire depository status have not had much success. While officials expressed interest in the idea, they felt that it would not be possible to arrange because of the difficulties of communicating between departments and the problems imposed by the decentralized system of distribution. Some librarians feel that this official reluctance was also due to a tendency to keep many reports confidential. They reported too that civil servants are often unaware of the library's role. "You have to spend a good deal of time proving that you need the documents." The Gosling Memorial Library also reported difficulties with present arrangements.

Other libraries seeking designation report that they receive full co-operation from the distributing agencies as far as materials intended for wide circulation are concerned. They hope, however, to avoid the time-consuming and costly method of following a complete order procedure for every item published. In other words, they wish to bring about automatic deposit, an ambition existing depositories have found unrealizable because of the decentralized structure of distribution facilities and the rapid turnover of the staff responsible for distribution. A few illustrations follow:

We sent a letter to all departments explaining that the Legislative Library is a depository. It was addressed to the Ministers who never passed it on to their underlings.

The problem of getting things is always underestimated by the Minister. He just says, "Oh! I'll send a letter around."

Mr Peel asked Mr Manning to make the University of Alberta library a depository. Mr Manning said he would send a memo to all Heads of Departments. There was no objection to making the library a depository. However, there was little result. Staff changes in the departments, or they forget and we must appeal to all the departments again.

Dalhousie University, with the assistance of the Atlantic Province's Library Association, has been seeking designation as a depository for Nova Scotia government publications, a request that has had a friendly reception from provincial officials but that, in the view of one official, is almost impossible to meet because of the highly decentralized distribution structure for Nova Scotian publications.

The difficulties experienced by university and public libraries are not always fully appreciated by governmental librarians. Following the 1966 resolution of the Canadian Political Science Association on the need for university depositories, one legislative librarian commented that "official provincial publications are sent ... to the other provinces on an exchange basis, therefore, there should be no problem about this."[18] A second legislative librarian also maintained that existing exchange arrangements between legislative libraries constituted all that is needed in a depository system. Unfortunately, the existing system is far from adequate. It does not ensure that all relevant public documents of a province are available in one collection, and it does not guarantee access to materials on the part of the general public or of scholars. Although the latter point has not been discussed in this chapter, it is an important argument in favour of revising the current system. For although most legislative libraries are usually open to the public and students, their lack of staff and frequently cramped quarters discourage such use when the legislature is in session. Hence, for a good portion of the year, their collections are not always open to outsiders. This is a problem that can be solved by the establishment of an effective depository system.

It should be noted that not all libraries would make the same demands of a depository system. The needs of the National Library of Canada and those of a regional public library would be quite different. The one has a responsibility to acquire the most complete collection that is possible of all provinces' documents, the other might wish to acquire only the type of statutory publications currently available from the relevant government libraries. Similarly, not every university library would wish to build an extensive research collection of provincial documents. Some do, however, as do some public libraries, and efforts must be made to discover a distribution formula that will meet their needs as well as the needs of those that are more easily satisfied.

CONCLUSIONS

The highly detailed material that has been presented in the last two chapters has served to illustrate the chaos that exists in the field of provincial document distribution. In none of the provinces, not even those with the most highly developed and most highly centralized systems, is the task of acquiring provincial publications an easy one. The frustrations facing the librarian, the scholar, and the average member of the public whom governments are supposed to serve are monumental and increase daily. The cost to the public cannot be measured, but in view of the waste that occurs in government and in the universities as a result of this system, together with the loss of savings that would result from a more complete dissemination of information, we must conclude that this too must be monumental.

These chapters have sought simply to describe. Some ways of overcoming the problem are suggested, but an approach to a properly integrated solution must be presented at a later stage of this study, in a somewhat broader context.

NOTES

1 / Interview with Mr J. Meredith, British Columbia Bureau of Economics and Statistics.
2 / Interview with Mr W. Hyrak, University of Alberta.
3 / The Newfoundland Legislative Library and the Alberta Provincial Library indicated that they possess depository status but did not provide documentation outlining precisely the scope accorded this status. The Quebec universities and the Quebec Legislative Library are recognized as depositories by the Quebec Official Printer and the University of Manitoba Library by the Manitoba Legislative Library, which distributes deposit documents. New Brunswick University libraries are recognized as depositories by NB - Order in Council 56-596; University of British Columbia library is believed to have been accorded depository status by a similar order in council of British Columbia in 1943. The current legislative authorizations for the remaining libraries are: Newfoundland Provincial Archives - Directive, Premier of Newfoundland to Ministers of all Government Departments, 21, January 1960: Legislative Library of Nova Scotia, Management Manual, Bulletin, 10P-31, 17, January 1967; New Brunswick Legislative Library, Order in Council 66-1042; Quebec National Library, *Quebec National Library Act*, 15-16 Elizabeth II, (1967-8) c.24; Provincial Library of Manitoba, Order in Council 1031/52; British Columbia Provincial Library, Order in Council of 25 Sept. 1961. These legislative authorizations have been reproduced in Appendix II.
4 / Latter part of definition adapted from NS Management Manual, Bulletin 10P-31. The definition has not discussed the problem of whether or not the library should pay for depository status. As a general rule deposit involves a payment in kind, recognition of an obligation to serve the public by preserving and making available the publications of the government concerned. However, in some instances governments and libraries might prefer to agree on a fixed charge for such status. This might be particularly relevant in the Canadian situation where a provincial government might wish to confine deposit to its own universities and legislative libraries of other governments, but might include major research libraries if they agreed to pay a fee.
5 / NB Order in Council 66-1042.
6 / Manitoba Order in Council 1031-52.
7 / Interview with Mrs S. Dodson, Government Documents Librarian, Universtiy of British Columbia Library.
8 / Interview with Mr A.M. Fraser, Provincial Archivist.
9 / Letter, M. Boone, Legislative Librarian, to R.G. Prodrick, Chairman, Government Publications Committee, Ontario Library Association, 30 Oct. 1962.
10 / NB Order in Council 52-1448.
11 / Boone to Prodrick.
12 / Interview with Miss M.H.G. Ashley.

13 / Interview with Miss C. Kollar, Government Documents Librarian, McGill University.
14 / *Report*, p.4
15 / *Ibid.*
16 / *Ibid.*, p. 6
17 / Ontario Legislative Assembly. *Memo re Tabling of Reports in the Legislative Library*, 2 May 1965. Provides that the Legislative Library receive two copies of every report tabled in the Legislature.
18 / Letter, E. Holmgren to S. Clarkson, Secretary-Treasurer, Canadian Political Science Association.

6
Finding aids: uncertain guides to publication production

The documents librarian building a research collection of provincial government publications can expect little assistance from the finding aids customarily used as tools for collection development. Such guideposts are sparse at the best of times and for some jurisdictions are almost non-existent. Instead, the librarian must rely on his own inventiveness and perseverance to discover, locate, and acquire the documents he needs.

In some libraries, notably the legislative libraries, long experience in the field has developed procedures that have proven effective in building collections. A compilation of these is presented in the first part of this chapter, together with some general comments that may be of assistance to the recent graduate who, possibly unexpectedly, finds himself in charge of the documents collection. The second part of the chapter presents a compendium of existing finding aids.

DOCUMENT DISCOVERY

Document discovery, the process whereby the librarian ascertains the existence of a document, precedes citation in any check-list, bibliography, or other finding aid. There are few aspects of librarianship demanding greater ingenuity and patience than the discovery of provincial government documents. Although specific jurisdictions possess unique administrative structures that will require development of special discovery techniques, the following procedures, an amalgam of those used by various libraries, are believed to be fairly generally applicable. Most procedures originate in the legislative libraries, but can be modified, as is suggested, for more general use. In each of the legislative libraries some or all of the following are used:
1 Where applicable, departments are periodically reminded that the library has depository status and departmental co-operation in depositing documents would be appreciated. Where depository status has not been accorded, the library can

explain its needs and thank the agency for co-operation given in the past. The technique has to be used with care and tact as departments already co-operating have sometimes reacted adversely to such a reminder.

2 Personal relationships are established with the secretaries of key officials and with staff handling documents for distribution. Although co-operation at this level is extremely helpful it is a long way from guaranteeing deposit. Staff turnover within the departments is high at the clerical level; most legislative librarians complained that they could not keep pace with the changes.

3 Official use of the library is watched with interest and where research patterns suggest that a document will be the result efforts are made to secure a copy. This is a *quid pro quo* arrangement and seems to work well where the library has succeeded in establishing its importance as a research centre. Unfortunately, for reasons which will be discussed at a later point, too few administrators are aware of the legislative library's resources and consequently seldom make the initial contact the library needs, both to prove itself and to obtain information concerning work in progress. Those university libraries extensively used by local bureaucracies are also in a position to obtain this sort of information.

4 The local newspapers are usually examined carefully for mention of release to the press of government studies. The fact that the press has received a copy does not ensure that the library has. Similarly, reference may be made to studies in progress.

5 Proceedings and debates of the legislature are followed (a) to ensure that a complete collection of tabled documents is maintained, and (b) to catch any reference that may be made to ongoing governmental studies.

6 Administrative documents are examined for reference to other documents not included in the collection and to projects in progress that may yield public reports.

7 Finally, legislative librarians sometimes employ the stratagems of the secret agent to improve their collections. In one jurisdiction the librarians are always one jump ahead of the char ladies, moving into their legislative chamber as soon as debate has adjourned, to search desk tops and wastepaper baskets for discarded documents. Visits to administrative offices provide clues to the existence of publications and efforts are made to secure copies for the library.

Some of these techniques are not open to use by the university and public librarian. The majority, perhaps with some modifications, are, however.

Daunting though the lack of finding aids may appear to the inexperienced documents librarian, he is equally disturbed by his complete ignorance of the bureaucratic structure he must thoroughly understand if he is to build a sound research collection. A number of documents librarians expressed their sense of inadequacy on this point, and we were struck by the fact that for many their work would have been much easier if their training had included a good introductory course in the structure of the provincial governments or even of the federal government. Unfortunately, some library schools do not offer a course in government documents for the first professional degree. In the courses that are offered, there may be a tendency to concentrate on the use of finding aids rather than on an understanding of the issuing agencies themselves. This is understandable and, for most aspects of librarianship, probably the only viable technique. Here, however, as in many other respects, the government documents situation can claim a different treatment. The documents librarian, more than most librarians concerned with acquisition, must possess a thorough understanding not only of which issuing agencies exist, but of how they work, if he is to achieve adequate results. Because of this, government documents librarians might be well advised to add to their library-school training one or two courses dealing with the structure of provincial governments and with public administration in general. Libraries might encourage their staff to undertake such additional specialized training, and library schools might permit such courses as options in the B.L.S. or M.L.S. programs. For the librarian forced to acquire on-the-job training, the following comments might prove helpful.

There are extremely few full-length monographs that deal with the structure of the provincial governments. Five that have been published are Frank MacKinnon, *The Government of Prince Edward Island*,[1] J.M. Beck, *The Government of Nova Scotia*,[2] M.S. Donnelly, *The Government of Manitoba*,[3] F. Schindeler, *Responsible Government in Ontario*,[4] and Andrée Lajoie, *Les Structures administratives régionales: déconcentration et décentralisation au Québec*.[5] Only the last of these deals at any length with descriptions of the administrative structure and process; nevertheless, they provide general background material which should be of help in interpreting the often cryptic comments found in the royal commission and management studies, which are the next best sources of information. The reports of public enquiries include *Report of the Committee on the Organization of Government in Ontario*,[6] and the Saskatchewan Royal Commission on Government Administration, *Report.*[7]

Reports prepared by consultants are often difficult to obtain as they are treated as confidential. However, some, such as the series of reports on government organization in Nova Scotia prepared in 1959 by Jerome Barnum Associates,[8] are available in university or legislative library collections. A few learned journals, particularly *Canadian Public Administration* and regional journals, such as *Ontario History* and *Dalhousie Review*, occasionally include articles on provincial matters. Finally, some assistance can be obtained from graduate theses in history and political science. Provincial studies are favoured particularly by Master's students, on the unjustified assumption that they are "less complicated" than federal studies and because research data frequently lie ready to hand.

Several governments issue administrative guides and yearbooks, which can be of great assistance both in researching and understanding government structure and as a finding aid. These include *Bottin administratif du Québec*,[9] and the *Quebec Year Book*,[10] edited by the Quebec Bureau of Statistics; *Directory and*

Guide to Services of the Government of Ontario;[11] Saskatchewan Budget Bureau, *Government of Saskatchewan-Organization and Functions;*[12] and Alberta Human Resources Research and Development Agency, *Inventory of Services for the Individual and the Community.* In a few instances provincial management manuals have been issued (and maintained) for use in research collections. Acquisition of this tool usually follows protracted negotiation with the treasury branch of the government concerned.

A valuable source of information, frequently overlooked because its use is extremely time-consuming, is the departmental annual report. The report will invariably include an organization chart, a formal description of the agency's functions, and references to specific projects about which the librarian may be anxious to learn more. In addition, some departments issue brief administrative guides to their own work (e.g., *Alberta Department of Agriculture: Its Functions and Services;*[13] Ontario Department of Lands and Forests, *A Statistical Reference of Lands and Forests Administration*[14]). A series of studies of structures of provincial departments to supplement *Canadiana* was never completed, although some agencies in Alberta, Manitoba, New Brunswick, Newfoundland, Ontario, Prince Edward Island, and Saskatchewan were described.

Finally, skeletal outlines of governmental structures can be derived from almanacs, the *Canada Year Book,*[15] and telephone directories. Most governments publish internal telephone directories, which are sometimes available to libraries. They are (information in brackets refers to the agency responsible for issuing the directory): Newfoundland (Department of Supply); Prince Edward Island; Nova Scotia; New Brunswick; Quebec (Minister of Public Works, Quebec Official Publisher); Ontario (Department of Public Works, Queen's Printer and Publisher); Manitoba; Saskatchewan (Office of Supply); and British Columbia. Fairly complete listings will be found in the public telephone directories of several provincial capitals.

In conclusion, it should be remembered that the procedures sketched here represent an ideal. Few libraries can afford the expense of carrying out a program of discovery such as has just been described. Furthermore, some of the procedures may only be practicable for libraries dealing with a government located in the same city. Nevertheless, it is hoped that some of the suggestions will be helpful.

CANADIANA

Since 1953, when it first began listing provincial government publications, *Canadiana* has become the most widely used finding aid in this field. Very frequently, because librarians lack the time for protracted correspondence with a multitude of distributing agencies, it is the only finding aid used for out-of-province publications. It describes documents from all provinces on a monthly basis, and potentially eliminates the need to study the numerous current departmental check-lists mentioned in this chapter. However, two major factors are said to limit this potential: the listing of provincial materials is incomplete and a time lag exists between publication of a document and its listing in *Canadiana*.

Canadiana is, in effect, a monthly catalogue of the publications deposited in the National Library of Canada. It is, then, only as complete as the National collection, which in turn is as complete as depositors care to make it. Incompleteness is a definite feature of the provincial government publications listings for two reasons. (a) Not all librarians agree on a definition of what should be deposited. Here we refer to the argument concerning the nature of the processed document. This has already been discussed and will not be further dealt with here. (b) Where the provincial legislative library supplies the national collection, the latter stands a reasonable chance of receiving the most important documents, but where the National Library must forage for itself, the collection, and thus the listing in *Canadiana*, is apt to be no more reliable than that of the average university library. Table 6:1 is a list of the National Library's suppliers in each of the provinces with the Library's estimate of their particular strengths.*

As the Library's own estimate suggests, there are notable weaknesses in the system. These might be overcome in part if the National Library could initiate discussions leading to agreement on a definition of a provincial government publication and if it could help the legislative libraries attain more complete reporting. This could be achieved through reimbursing the legislative libraries for the considerable service they now provide to the federal institution. Such payments could be used to hire the personnel needed to carry out a more effective discovery and acquisitions program.

The second difficulty reported by some librarians may not be as important, at present, as a few have suggested. This is the question of time lag. Some librarians note that documents are reported in *Canadiana* a considerable time after they have been released to the public and suggest that the danger of ordering out-of-print items is quite high. Although this may be true of publications issued by the Atlantic region governments, where print runs are short, and could certainly be true if more processed documents were reported, the survey located very few instances of documents being out of print by the time they were reported in *Canadiana*. Some evidence suggested that documents are processed reasonably quickly. Mr Maurice Boone, Legislative Librarian of New Brunswick, reported that items received by him in February 1968 and deposited at the National Library within two weeks, were reported in the April edition of

*In two instances, this account differs from that we received in the provinces. Alberta's Provincial Librarian reported that the Provincial Library sends some material but most departments send their own; the Legislative Librarian in Prince Edward Island reported that he sends the province's publications to the National Library every year at the end of the legislative session.

TABLE 6:1
Sources of provincial publications listed in **Canadiana**

Alberta: very good
    Provincial library (main source)
    Alberta Oil and Gas Conservation Board (sends us everything)
    Alberta Research Council (almost everything)
    some departmental periodicals

British Columbia: very good
    Provincial library (main source)
    British Columbia Research Council (good)
    some crown corporations

Manitoba: very good
    Provincial library (main source)
    Department of Health and Welfare Library (quite a bit)
    some departmental periodicals

New Brunswick: very good
    Legislative library (main source)
    some departmental periodicals

Newfoundland: good
    Departments (mainly annual reports)
    Queen's Printer (statutes, public accounts)

Nova Scotia: good
    Queen's Printer (annual reports, statutes, public accounts)
    some departments

Prince Edward Island: good
    Departments (mainly annual reports)

Ontario: fair
    Legislative library (sessional papers only)
    Departments (three-quarters of them)

Quebec: good
    Legislative library
    Official publisher
    some departments

Saskatchewan: very good
    Legislative library (main source)
    some periodicals

Canadiana, which appeared in late May. A three-month time lag is quite respectable. Similarly, a comparison of *Canadiana* and the listings in the *B.C.L.A. Reporter* revealed that documents appeared in both publications almost simultaneously.

However, while these admittedly scanty findings tend to support the current listing procedure, some consideration might be given to making proof sheets available to libraries on the same basis as proof sheets are distributed for Part I of *Canadiana*. Such a procedure should certainly be introduced if processed documents are to be listed.

BIBLIOGRAPHIES AND CHECK-LISTS OF PROVINCIAL PUBLICATIONS

The chaotic state of provincial government publishing is perhaps epitomized by the condition of the field's bibliographic resources. There are a surprisingly large number of bibliographies and check-lists of provincial documents, but far too many are redundant, incomplete, obscure, and often difficult to obtain. André Beaulieu comments:

Comme dans d'autres secteurs - ceux de l'édition et de la diffusion par exemple - il y a d'abord beaucoup d'efforts inutiles et de double emploi. En effet, un net manque de planification et de coordination semble être monnaie courante. Est-il normal que de nombreux départements ou services de ministères publient sporadiquement ou régulièrement des listes bibliographiques, alors que tel autre service ou tel autre département ne peut pas faire de même? Parfois encore un ministère publie la liste de ses publications et tel autre pas. D'où, bien sûr, un éventail hétéroclite qui le plus souvent confond plus qu'il n'informe l'usager.

Il en est ainsi dans la province de Québec. Services et ministères publient différents types de liste bibliographique - ouvrages publiés, ouvrages vendus, ouvrages distribués - sans que nous ayions une source sûre d'identification.[16]

This compilation of bibliographies and other lists that contain provincial government documents is intended as an aid to those trying to acquire them under the present system. It has been compiled with the help of many people working in the field. Although it attempts to draw together all known finding aids,* it doubtless covers only a small part of what exists but is hidden in the labyrinths of government. Information for the list was collected during interviews in 1968, and after follow-up correspondence. Use was made of

---

*Some have been omitted where their contents have been included in later, more general works: for instance, the *List of Royal Commissions, Special Reports, etc., Pertaining to the Province of Saskatchewan* compiled at the Saskatchewan Legislative Library in 1947, was incorporated in Christine MacDonald's *Publications of the Governments of the Northwest Territories ... and of the Province of Saskatchewan ...*

Raymond Tanghe's *Bibliography of Canadian Bibliographies* (Toronto, University of Toronto Press for Société bibliographique du Canada, 1960). The list was completed in August 1969, but with the appearance of Mohan Bhatia's *Bibliographies, Catalogues, Checklists and Indexes of Canadian Provincial Government Publications* (Saskatoon, University of Saskatchewan, Saskatoon Library, 1970) it was amended slightly. Generally, later publications that have been brought to our attention have been entered in footnotes.

GENERAL

Boult, Reynald. *Bibliographie du droit canadien*. Montreal: Wilson et Lafleur, 1966. 393 pp.
Contains a more up-to-date list of Canadian statutes and regulations than *A Legal Bibliography of the British Commonwealth of Nations*, cited below.

Brown, C.R., P.A. Maxwell, and L.F. Maxwell. *A Legal Bibliography of the British Commonwealth of Nations*, vol. 3, *Canadian and British American Colonial Law, From Earliest Times to December 1956*. London: Sweet and Maxwell, 1957. 218 pp.

Buchanan, Sue. *Canadian Federal and Provincial Royal Commissions; Holdings U.B.C. Library*. Vancouver, July 1968. Unpublished.

Canada Year Book; Official Statistical Annual of the Resources, History, Institutions and Social and Economic Conditions of Canada, 1905. Ottawa: Dominion Bureau of Statistics, 1906.
Informs of some studies underway in the various provinces. Mentioned some provincial publications from 1914-46. In 1940 it backlisted a number of provincial royal commissions to 1870 and has listed some annually ever since.

Canadian Council of Resource Ministers. *Report*. Montreal: the Council. Annual.
Contains descriptions of the Council's publications, including two periodicals begun in 1968-9: *Sources*, a compendium of recent articles and speeches on renewable resource development in Canada, and *References*, a compilation of resource references, book reviews, and recent legislation.

Canadiana, 1950. Ottawa: National Library of Canada, 1953. Monthly.
See description, pages 65-68.

Carleton University Library. *Selected List of Current Materials on Canadian Public Administration and Political Science*. No. 19, February 1965.
Contains a fair number of government documents.

Current publications in Legal and Related Fields, 1953. South Hackensak, N.J.:
F. B. Rothman for American Association of Law Libraries.
Since February 1968, the "Checklist of Current State, Federal and Canadian Publications," compiled by Frances K. Holbrook and formerly published in the *Law Library Journal* has appeared in the February and August issues. Selective.

Dalhousie University. Institute of Public Affairs. Municipal Reference Library. Accessions. 1957, 1969, 1970.
These include publications of various provinces on public administration.

Gregory, Winnifred. *List of the Serial Publications of Foreign Governments, 1815-1931.* New York: Wilson, 1932.
Includes a large number of Canadian provincial documents and locates copies in Canadian and American libraries.

Canadian Library Association. Government Reference Libraries Committee. *Provincial Royal Commissions.*
Listings provided from each province are in the hands of the general editor, Mr Eric Holmgren.

Johnson, George. *Regulations Under Dominion and Provincial Statutes and How to Locate Them.* 2 pp. mimeo.

Lande, Lawrence. *The Lawrence Lande Collection of Canadiana in the Redpath Library of McGill University; a Bibliography.* Montreal: Lawrence Lande Foundation for Canadian Historical Research, 1965.
Contains a few provincial documents.

Liboiron, Albert A. *Federalism and Intergovernmental Relations in Australia, Canada, and the United States and Other Countries; a bibliography.* Kingston, Ontario: Institute of Intergovernmental Relations, Queen's University, 1967. 231 pp.
A rich source of references to provincial documents.

New York. Public Library. *Catalog of Government Documents, Economics Division, the Research Libraries of the New York Public Library.* 1967. 40 vols.

Toronto. Public Library. *A Bibliography of Canadiana.* Toronto, 1934. 828 pp. Supplement 1959.
Lists all Canadian imprints up to 1867 in Toronto Public Library's collection, including government publications.

Toronto. Public Library. *The Canadian Catalogue of Books Published in Canada, about Canada, as Well as Those Written by Canadians with Imprint 1921-1949. Consolidated English Language Reprint with Cumulated Author Index.* Toronto, 1959. 2 vols.
Includes selected provincial government publications.

Tremaine, Marie. *A Bibliography of Canadian Imprints, 1751-1800.* Toronto, University of Toronto Press, 1952. 705 pp.
Describes publications of the various governments of the time.

U. S. Library of Congress. *A Catalog of Books Represented by Library of Congress Printed Cards Issued to July 31, 1942.* Ann Arbor, Mich.: Edwards, 1942-6. 167 vols.
Most useful of Library of Congress catalogs for provincial documents. *Canadiana* now contains more.

Urban & Regional References Urbanes & Regionales 1945-62. Ottawa: Canadian Council of Urban and Regional Research, 1964. Supplements 1963-64; 1965-66; 1967.
Some items in first volumes not listed in *Canadiana*. Provides a subject approach.

REGIONAL

Atlantic Provinces Checklist, 1957. Halifax: Atlantic Provinces Library Association in co-operation with Atlantic Provinces Economic Council, 1958.
Includes government publications except annual reports of departments.

Atlantic Provinces Economic Council. *Bibliography of Research Projects.* Fredericton, N. B.: Atlantic Provinces Research Board, 1965. Annual.
Concerned with economic research done in or related to the Atlantic Provinces. Compilers able to include little of Atlantic Development Board research or *ad hoc* research done for governments by consultants which is held as confidential to government.

Bishop, Olga Bernice. *Publications of the Governments of Nova Scotia, Prince Edward Island, New Brunswick, 1758-1952.* Ottawa: National Library, 1957. 237 pp.

Bishop, Olga Bernice. *Publications of the Government of the Province of Canada, 1841-1867.* Ottawa: National Library of Canada, 1963. 351 pp.

Dalhousie University. Institute of Public Affairs. *Royal Commission Reports and*

Related Action, 1926-1960. Halifax: the Institute for Atlantic Provinces Economic Council, 1969. 173 pp. Institute publications No. 19.

Edmondson, Locksley G. *Canadian Provincial Royal Commissions. New Brunswick, Newfoundland, Prince Edward Island.* 1962. 124 pp.
Includes royal commissions established since entry into Confederation to 1960. Copies obtainable at Government Documents Division, Douglas Library, Queen's University.

PROVINCIAL

*Newfoundland**

Newfoundland. Dept. of Mines, Agriculture and Resources. Mineral Resources Division. *List of publications.* 1968. 5 pp.
Lists material published since 1934. Out-of-print material mentioned can be reproduced at cost by the Division on request. Check-list updated periodically. A list of the Division's publications also appears in the Department's annual report.

O'Dea, Agnes. *A Newfoundland Bibliography.* St. John's, Newfoundland: Memorial University.
This bibliography is to include books, pamphlets and periodical articles relating to Newfoundland, including provincial documents, to 1960. Publication date is not yet known.

Nova Scotia

Nova Scotia. Legislative Library. *A Finding List of Royal Commissions Appointed by the Province of Nova Scotia 1877-1965.* 9 1.
Notes date of appointment, hearings, date of report, and commissioners of each.

Nova Scotia. Legislative Library. *Publications of the Province of Nova Scotia, 1967.* Halifax: Queen's Printer, 1968. Annual.

New Brunswick

New Brunswick. Dept. of Agriculture and Rural Development. *Publications*

---

*Newfoundland. Dept. of Mines, Agriculture and Resources. Mineral Resource, Division. Bibliography of the Geology of Newfoundland and Labrador 1814 through 1968, by J. Butler and E. Bartlett. St. John's, Nfld., the Dept., 1970.

available, February 1968. 7 1.
Includes material published by each branch. Revised annually.

New Brunswick. Dept. of Natural Resources. Publications. (n.d.) 21.

New Brunswick. Department of Natural Resources. Mineral Resources Branch. *List of Publications Available* ... by R.R. Potter. 1968. (Information Circular no. 68-2)

New Brunswick. Dept. of Natural Resources. Surveys Branch. Maps available for sale and price list. (n.d.) 1 p.

New Brunswick. Legislative Library. *New Brunswick Government Documents. A Checklist of New Brunswick Government Documents Received at the Legislative Library, Fredericton, N.B., During the Calendar Year* ... Fredericton, N.B., 1955.
Since 1952 the Queen's Printer of New Brunswick has been required by order-in-council to deposit in the New Brunswick Legislative Library copies of anything printed under the Queen's Printer Act, i.e., statutory documents or documents ordered to be printed, by the Lieutenant Governor-in-Council. This check-list, however, includes many documents besides those deposited by the Queen's Printer.

New Brunswick. Provincial Archives. *Checklist of Secondary Sources for the History of New Brunswick,* unpublished.
A check-list compiled by Provincial Archivist, H.H. Taylor, which includes government publications of a special nature and of considerable historic content such as royal commissions. Although these may be recorded in Bishop's work, information is given in this check-list as to their location.

Prince Edward Island

Prince Edward Island, Legislative Library. *Significant Publications of the Government of Prince Edward Island, 1967-68.* 4 1.

Quebec

Beaulieu, André, Jean-Charles Bonenfant, et Jean Hamelin. *Répertoire de publications gouvernementales du Québec. 1867-1967.* Québec: Imprimeur de la Reine, 1968. 554 pp.*

*A supplement for 1965-1968 was scheduled to appear in 1970.

Garigue, Philippe. *Bibliographie du Québec, 1955-65.* Supplement: *Canadian Journal of Political Science,* vol. 1, no. 1 (March 1968), pp. 107-18.

The supplement includes a section devoted to Quebec publications, although the original bibliography does not. Further up-datings are promised in subsequent issues of the *Canadian Journal of Political Science.*

Hamilton, R.M. *Quebec Government Publications to 1841.* (In *Ontario Library Review,* May 1938, pp. 1-3)

Québec. Bibliothèque Nationale. *Bibliographie du Québec.* Montréal: la Bibliothèque, 1969. Trimestriel.

This bibliography of current publications published in or related to Quebec includes a section devoted to the provincial government's publications.

Québec. Dept. of Natural Resources. *Aeromagnetic Maps.* Québec: the Department, 1964. English and French. 2 pp.

Québec. Ministère de l'Agriculture et de la Colonisation. Service de la Récherche. *Division des Renseignements Scientifiques. Liste des publications.* Québec: le Ministère, 1966. Publication 281. 6 pp.

Québec. Ministère de l'Education. Service d'information. *Publications.* No. 1, mars 1968.

Québec. Ministère de la Famille et du Bien-Etre Social. Service de l'Information. *Liste des lois et documents qui sont à la disposition de public.* 2 pp.

Québec. Ministère de l'Industrie et du Commerce. *Liste des publications.* 1968. 13 f.

Québec. Ministère de l'Industrie et du Commerce. *Industries manufacturières* (n.d.) 23 f.

Names lists available of industries and manufacturers in the province.

Québec. Ministère de la Santé. Service de l'Education Sanitaire. *Liste des imprimes.* 8 pp.

Québec. Ministère de la Santé. Service de l'Education Sanitaire. *Liste des imprimes techniques.* 4 pp.

Québec. Ministère du Tourisme, de la Chasse, et de la Pêche. Service de la Faune. *Bulletins.* 2 pp.

Quebec. Queen's Printer. *Publications on sale at the office of the Queen's Printer, Parliament Buildings, Quebec.* 1966. 1967.
Started ambitiously with the intention of expanding to list all Quebec publications, both free and for sale, but financial problems have intervened.

Ontario

Bishop, Olga Bernice, ed.
Professor Bishop has received grants from the Midwestern Regional Library System to support the compilation of a check-list of Ontario publications between 1867 and 1900. Effort is being concentrated on publications of the Legislature, Departments of Attorney-General, Provincial Secretary, Crown Lands, Public Works, Health, Mines, Agriculture, Education, and on publications of royal commissions. The work is in progress.

Bucksar, R.G. *Bibliography of Socio-Economic Development of Northern Ontario (North-western and North-eastern regions).* Ottawa: Canadian Research Centre for Anthropology, 1968. 112 pp.

Dwivedi, O.P. *Administration of the Public Personnel Functions in the Province of Ontario.* 1968. 314 l. Bibliography: leaves 305-14.
Bibliography deals with personnel administration in Ontario, 1901-66 and includes provincial documents. Available from the National Library and as No. 1866 of the Canadian Theses on Microfilm series.

Harris, Robin S. *A List of Reports to the Legislature of Ontario Bearing on Higher Education in the Province.* Comp. by Robin S. Harris with the assistance of Constance Allen and Mary Lewis. Toronto: Innis College, University of Toronto, 1966. 17 pp.

Harris, Robin S. *An Annotated List of the Legislative Acts Concerning Higher Education in Ontario.* Comp. by Robin S. Harris with the assistance of Constance Allen and Mary Lewis. Toronto: Innis College, University of Toronto, 1966. 79 pp.

MacTaggart, Hazel. *Publications of the Government of Ontario, 1905-1955.* Toronto: University of Toronto Press for the Queen's Printer, 1964. 303 pp.

Ontario. Department of Agriculture and Food. *Publications.* Toronto: the Department. Annual.
Items listed are intended for general distribution.

Ontario. Department of Agriculture and Food. Farm Economics, Co-operatives

and Statistics Branch. *A Selective List of Available Publications.* Toronto: the Branch, 1968. 4 1.
A list of research reports not included in the above brochure. Intended for interested people in the Department and others in the specialized field.

Ontario. Department of Agriculture and Food. Information Branch. *New Publications.* Bi-monthly.

Ontario. Department of Economics and Development. *Publications.* (n.d.) 2 pp.

Ontario. Department of Economics and Development. Office of the Chief Economist. Economic Analysis Branch. *Economic Reports; a Selected Bibliography of Economic Reports Produced by Ontario Government Departments.* March, September, 1967.

Ontario. Department of Education. *Report.* Annual.
Most of the Department's publications are listed here.

Ontario. Department of Energy and Resources Management. *List of Geological Reports of Ontario.* Revised 1968. Toronto, 1968.

Ontario. Department of Energy and Resources Management. Petroleum Resources Section. *List of Publications and Maps.* Toronto, 1968. 6 pp.

Ontario. Department of Highways. *Historical Chronology of Highway Legislation in Ontario 1774-1961.* Comp. and summarized by Irma E. Pattison. 1964.

Ontario. Department of Highways. Research Branch. *List of Reports Available ...* (n.d.) 25, 12 1. mimeo.
Once this list has been sent, the Research Branch promises to send brief summaries of new research reports as they become available.

Ontario. Department of Lands and Forests. *Publications 1968-69.* 6 pp.
This brochure notes: "For professional workers, advanced students and active conservationists, reports and scientific papers are available in limited quantities from Fish and Wildlife Branch and from Research Branch ... Enquiries on Silviculture or forest trees should be directed to Timber Branch." One page is devoted to listing other agencies that may distribute relevant information. The brochure omits several publications listed in the 1968 annual report of the Department under Conservation Information Section of Operations Branch and under Research Branch.

Ontario. Department of Mines. *Publications Price List.* April 1968.

Ontario. Department of Municipal Affairs. *Library Bulletin.* Weekly or more frequent.
The accessions lists that appear here are the most complete up-to-date listings available for Ontario. Serials are included.

Ontario. Department of Tourism and Information. *Directory and Guide to Services of the Government of Ontario.* Toronto: the Department. Annual.*
Includes a very selective list of Ontario documents. Publications dates are often omitted. Not published in 1968 or 1969.

Ontario. Department of Revenue. *Packing Slip.* 1 p.
An invoice of documents distributed by the Department.

Ontario. Department of Revenue. Travel Research Branch. *Travel Research Reports: Abstracts 1967-1968.*

Ontario. Queen's Printer. *Ontario Gazette.*
A list of publications offered for sale by the Queen's Printer appears each week.†

Smith, R.P. *Royal Commissions of the Province of Ontario 1867 to 1950.* 1960. 43 1.
Deposited in the Local Government Library, Queen's University.

Ontario. Economic Council. *Publications.* 1969. 1 p.

Ontario. Economic Council. *Research Index; Projects Being Carried on Within Ontario Government Departments and Agencies, and in a Number of Companies Operating in Ontario in Agriculture, Architecture, Chemistry, Earth Science, Physics, and a Summary of Reported Industrial Research Facilities.* Toronto. 1965. Annual.

Ontario. Legislative Library. *Bi-monthly Book List; a List of Books Acquired by*

*This publication became the responsibility of the Queen's Printer and Publisher in 1970 and is now entitled *Guide to Ontario Government Services.*
†In 1970 the *Ontario Government Publications Catalogue* (Toronto: Queen's Printer and Publisher, 493 pp.) appeared. It was an inventory of departmental publications taken from 1 November 1968 to 10 October 1969 and promised to be an annual publication kept up to date with monthly check-lists. It was subsequently withdrawn because of flaws. One major difficulty was that approaches to the entries were limited and imprecise.

the Legislative Library. New Series, 1965.
A selective list distributed to heads of government, deputies, librarians, and others who request it.

Spencer, Loraine, and Susan Holland, comps. *Northern Ontario: a Bibliography.* Toronto: University of Toronto Press, 1968.
Includes a few Ontario government publications.

Manitoba*

Manitoba. Department of Industry and Commerce. *Manitoba Fact Book.* (n.d.) 83 pp.
A listing of the Department's publications appears on pp. 81-3. It is revised for each new edition of *The Fact Book.*

Manitoba. Department of Mines and Natural Resources. Mines Branch. *Publication.*
Includes "Bibliography of geology of the Precambrian area of Manitoba, 1950-1957," compiled by G.S. Barry, 1959. Also includes "Bibliography of geology, palaeontology, industrial minerals, and fuels in the Post-Cambrian regions of Manitoba 1958 to 1965" compiled by B.B. Bannatyne. 1966.

Manitoba. Queen's Printer.
Answers enquiries with a letter describing what is on hand.

Morley, Marjorie. *A Bibliography of Manitoba from Holdings in the Legislative Library of Manitoba, September 1953.* 45 pp.
Includes some government publications.

Morley, Marjorie, ed. *Royal Commissions and Commissions of Enquiry Under "The Evidence Act" in Manitoba; a Checklist 1886-1949.* Winnipeg: Provincial Library, 1949. 9 pp.

Saskatchewan

MacDonald, Christine. *Publications of the Governments of the Northwest Territories, 1876-1905, and of the Province of Saskatchewan, 1905-1952.* Regina: Legislative Library, 1952. 109 pp.
Some royal commissions mentioned here do not appear in Buchanan's list and *vice versa.*

*Manitoba. Department of Agriculture. Economics and Publications Branch. *List of Publications.* Winnipeg: Queen's Printer, 1969.

Saskatchewan. Archives. *Guides to the Records of all Royal Commissions Appointed by the Province of Saskatchewan.* Comp. by John Nicks. 1964. Supplement, comp. by E.C. Morgan, 1968. Unpublished.
Both manuscripts are at the Archives.

Saskatchewan. Department of Agriculture. Agricultural Information Division. *Farm bulletins.* Regina, the Division. Annual.

Saskatchewan. Department of Education. *List of publications.* Annual.

Saskatchewan. Department of Mineral Resources. Mineral Records Branch. *Catalogue of Maps and Publications.* 1967. 116 pp.
Includes then currently available material.

Saskatchewan. Department of Municipal Affairs. Community Planning Branch. *Planning Reports and Studies Available, June 1969.* 5 pp.

Saskatchewan Research Council. *Reports, 1957-1968.* 1969. 19 pp.
This list is soon to be replaced by a computerized index of all the Council's publications, including university theses supported by the Council, on Cherry's Streamed Information System II.

Alberta

Alberta. Department of Agriculture. *List of publications 1967-68.* Edmonton: Queen's Printer, 1967. 24 pp.

Alberta. Department of Education. *Publications.* 6 pp. Annual.

Alberta. Department of Industry and Tourism. *Current Publications.* 1968.
A selective list issued periodically (about every four years).

Alberta. Human Resources Research and Development Agency. *Inventory of Services for the Individual and the Community.* (1968?) 4 vols.
For each service described, details on how to obtain more information from the Alberta government are given.

Alberta. Oil and Gas Conservation Board. *Catalogue of Publications, Services and Maps, 1964.* Calgary, 1964. Annual.

Alberta. Queen's Printer. *List of Publications Available.* (n.d.)

Alberta. Research Council. *List of publications 1969.* 1969. 34 pp.

Alberta. Research Council. Library. *List of Government Serials in the Documents Section, June 1967.*
Citations of provincial government serials are included.

Forsyth, J.
Mr Forsyth is engaged in compiling a bibliography of Alberta government documents as a thesis for the Library Association of Great Britain and hopes to complete it by 1970. He is presently working at the Calgary Public Library.

MacDonald, Christine. *Publications of the Governments of the Northwest Territories, 1876-1905, and of the Province of Saskatchewan, 1905-1952.* Regina: Legislative Library, 1952. 109 pp.
Includes Alberta material to 1905.

Within our borders. Edmonton. Monthly.
A newsletter describing government services which sometimes mentions in passing items which are or are about to be distributed. Available from Rm 245, Highways Building, Edmonton.

British Columbia*

British Columbia. Department of Agriculture. *List of Publications.* Revised 1967. Victoria: Queen's Printer, 1967. 5 pp.

British Columbia. Department of Education. Textbook Branch. *Programmes, manuals, etc. ... 1968.* 3 pp.

British Columbia. Department of Industrial Development, Trade and Commerce. *Publications.* Victoria: Queen's Printer. Annual.
Lists in-print and some popular out-of-print material. Not published for 1956 or 1958.

British Columbia. Department of Mines and Petroleum Resources. *List of Publications.* Victoria: Queen's Printer. Annual.

British Columbia. *Gazette.* Victoria: Queen's Printer, 1871.
Part II contains an annual price list of British Columbia statutes and

*British Columbia. Provincial Library. *Checklist of Publications Received from the British Columbia Government.* Monthly. U.B.C. Library News, vol. 3, no. 4 (April 1970) comments: "Virtually all provincial government publications including those meant only for departmental distribution. ... information on ordering is ... given."

regulations which is available separately on request. As royal commission reports are published and made available, Part I of the *Gazette* gives date, name of commissioner, and cost price under department responsible for the report.

British Columbia. Lower Mainland Regional Planning Board. *Publications List.* Vancouver, 1968. 20 pp.

British Columbia. Research Council. *Publications.* Vancouver: the Council at the University of British Columbia, 1964. 26 l.

B.C.L.A. Reporter; the Newsletter of the British Columbia Library Association, 1957. Monthly.
Contains "A Selection of Recent British Columbia Provincial Government Publications." This list is arranged by subject. Most entries appear at the same time in *Canadiana.*

Holmes, Marjorie C. *Publications of the Government of British Columbia, 1871-1947.* Victoria: Queen's Printer, 1950. 254 pp.
Since royal commissions before 1942 were recorded in her previous check-list mentioned below, only those after 1942 are included here. A further revision of this work is contemplated, perhaps to be published in 1971.

Holmes, Marjorie C. *Royal Commissions and Commissions of Inquiry Under the "Public Inquiries Act" in British Columbia, 1872-1942; a Checklist.* Victoria: King's Printer, 1945. 68 pp.

Lowther, Barbara. *Bibliography of British Columbia; Laying the Foundations 1849-1899.* Victoria: University of Victoria, 1968. 328 pp.
See index under B.C. and Vancouver Island for relevant items. Based mainly on collections in the B.C. Archives and in the Bancroft Library of California. Any documents already listed in Holmes are omitted.

NOTES

1 / Toronto: University of Toronto Press, 1951.
2 / Toronto: University of Toronto Press, 1957.
3 / Toronto: University of Toronto Press, 1965.
4 / Toronto: University of Toronto Press, 1969.
5 / Montreal: Presses de l'université de Montréal, 1968. André Gélinas, *Les Parlementaires et l'administration au Québec* (Québec: Presses de l'université Laval, 1969) also may be found useful. A project to compile an administrative history of the Province of Quebec has

been organized recently by the University of Montreal under the direction of Professor I. Gow. A study of the Saskatchewan government is being prepared for publication by Professor E. Eager.

6 / Toronto, 1959.
7 / Regina: Queen's Printer, 1965.
8 / A copy is available at the Killam Library, Dalhousie University.
9 / Québec: Office d'Information et de Publicité du Québec, n.d.
10 / Québec: Queen's Printer, 1965.
11 / Toronto: Department of Tourism and Information, 1967. Revised 1970 by the Queen's Printer and Publisher.
12 / Regina: Queen's Printer, 1959.
13 / Edmonton: Queen's Printer, 1959.
14 / Toronto: the Department, 1964.
15 / Ottawa: Queen's Printer.
16 / A. Beaulieu, *Le Rapport Pross et son contenu relatif au Québec* (ms. 1970).

7
Existing library resources

A major impediment to academic research into provincial problems has been the lack of information concerning the location of useful collections of provincial publications. At present few of these documents are listed in union catalogues, and bibliographies do not always record locations, so that the ratings of strength of collections found on the following pages may at least eliminate some of the guesswork and frustration from the business of tracking down desired sources.

A brief commentary also outlines the state of the country's holdings of provincial Hansards, royal commission materials, and electoral data. The very limited efforts made to date to microfilm provincial publications are reported and the problem of user access to collections is discussed.

STRENGTH OF COLLECTIONS

The questionnaires sent to libraries attempted a tentative and imprecise effort to gather comparative data concerning the extent and depth of holdings of provincial publications. Each library was asked to evaluate its holdings of debates, statutes, and departmental annual reports of all provinces.* These particular holdings were chosen because they are common to most provinces and the annual character makes gaps fairly obvious. Unfortunately, this approach failed to achieve a satisfactory measure of the strength or quality of collections. Because provincial government structures differ and are changing constantly, their publications seldom meet the demands of a standardized evaluation chart such as we put forward.† For instance, although a department may have been recently established, work in its jurisdiction may have a long history in the

---

*Legislative and Archival Libraries were asked to evaluate holdings of their own provinces' publications only.
†See Appendix I.

province. Alberta's Department of Lands and Forests was created in 1950 when the former Department of Natural Resources was split into the Department of Lands and Forests and the Department of Mines and Minerals. Manitoba's Department of Labor began as the Bureau of Labor under the Department of Public Works; Ontario's Department of Mines started life as the Bureau of Mines in the Department of Crown Lands. When a library evaluated its holdings of annual reports of these departments it was not necessarily referring to reports dealing with the same subjects issued before the formation of current agencies.

The usefulness of the evaluation is also affected by the fact that the most valuable documents are not always the ones most easily collected or assessed. Annual reports are much easier to collect and discuss on questionnaires than the vast array of research reports, royal commissions, educational materials, and the like, which are produced at irregular intervals and often distributed in haphazard fashion. But the contents of the latter are usually more valuable to the investigator. Therefore, the following comparisons of the data collected may accord unduly high ratings to libraries that have concentrated on building their serial publications collection but have paid little attention to processed and other irregularly published items.

The most serious problem confronted in this attempt at evaluation was the almost complete lack of standards against which individual collections could be measured. This problem will exist until sufficient bibliographies have been compiled to allow librarians to carry out the meticulous assessments needed.

Tables 7:1-10 present the data from the evaluations proposed in Questionnaires 3 and 4, and are arranged in geographical order, moving from east to west. The system of evaluation suggested to respondents, and fairly faithfully followed by them, is as follows:

A strong collections, nearly a complete run;
B good, more than ¾ of items actually issued;
C fair, ¼ to ½ of volumes actually issued;
D weak, less than ¼ of items actually issued;
O not represented in the collection.

Accompanying each chart is a brief commentary, which summarizes users comments on the over-all quality of the documents collections of the libraries within the province. These have a limited applicability. No standards for the judgments were suggested in the questionnaire, and it appears from some remarks that in a number of instances users were judging the output of a government as much as the strength and organization of a collection. Furthermore, the great range of user needs makes it difficult to assess the general applicability of their comments; strong retrospective collections would satisfy the historian, but the political scientist demands current publications.

The references to holdings of a given province's documents beyond the boundaries of that province are based on a reading of the tables. While the conditions we have described are bound to produce some variations in evaluation of holdings, other evidence suggests that the two libraries reporting the most extensive collections do in fact possess much better collections than any other academic or public libraries. It is no exaggeration to say that the University of British Columbia and Queen's University possess the only collections of provincial government documents outside of governmental libraries that are at all reliable for research purposes. In general, the state of affairs reported in these evaluations represented a national disgrace. The university collections in the Atlantic provinces are extremely weak, those on the prairies not much better. Quebec libraries report great weakness in out-of-province holdings.

Generally speaking, public libraries were not sent questionnaires. However, a few possess national or local reputations in the field and these were circulated and interviews were held with their staff. The Toronto Public Library is the only public library having a sizable collection of publications of all provinces. Its holdings would distinguish the libraries of most universities. The Gosling Memorial Library has a unique collection of Newfoundlandia, whilst the Calgary and the Vancouver public libraries also boast good collections of publications from their own provinces.

In all cases but Newfoundland's, the legislative library maintains a good research collection of materials relating to its own province. In some cases this collection is the only one of significance in the province. An irreparable blow could be struck to the historic fabric of the country should any one of these collections ever be damaged by fire.

The National Library of Canada has been collecting provincial publications since about the time of its organization in the early fifties and acquisitions of current material since then are recorded in *Canadiana*. The National Library's evaluations in the tables do not refer to pre-1953 material, although it has been given "a great deal" of this material by the Library of Parliament and others. Its aim is a complete collection for each province. The National Library is open to post-graduate students and to undergraduates and high-school students if they have a letter from their library stating exactly what material is needed and affirming that such material is not available in their own library.

The Parliamentary Library appears to have a very good retrospective collection of annual reports. Its main purpose is to serve Parliamentarians, but it is open to others on much the same terms as the National Library as long as service to MPs is not thereby curtailed.

Questionnaires were sent to four libraries in the United States that have some reputation for collections of Canadian material: the Library of Congress, Harvard University's Littauer Library, the New York Public Library, and the Library of Duke University. The two libraries that answered, the Library of Congress and Littauer, contain surprisingly little in this field.

TABLE 7:1

HOLDINGS OF NEWFOUNDLAND PUBLICATIONS

	Nfld. Leg. Lib.	Nfld. Archives	Mem. Univ. of Nfld.[8]	Dalhousie Univ. MacDonald Mem. Lib.	Dalhousie Univ. Sir J. Dunn Lib.	Univ. of NB Harriet Irving Lib.	McGill Univ. McLennan Lib.	Sir George Williams Univ.	Univ. de Montréal Main Lib.	Brock Univ. Main Lib.	Laurentian Univ. Laurentian Lib.	McMaster Univ. Mills Mem. Lib.
Debates	A		A									
Journals	A	A	A	C			D					
Sessional papers	A		A									
Statutes	A	C	A		B	D	D		C			D
Departmental annual reports:												
Agriculture	A	A	C			D					D	
Attorney-General[1]		A										
Education[2]	A	A	C	B		D	C	C	D			
Highways	A	A	C									
Labour		A	D									
Lands and Forests[3]	A	A	C									
Mining[4]	A	A	C				C	D		D	D	D
Municipal Affairs	A	A	A				D	D				
Provincial Secretary		A	D									
Public accounts[5]	*	*	C	C			D	D		D		D
Public Health and Welfare[6]	A	A	C	C			D	D	D			
Trade and Industry[7]	A	A										

1 No printed annual reports.
2 Printed 1928.
3 Printed 1954.
4 Including geology.
5 Printed 1919.
6 Printed 1946.
7 In Newfoundland the Department of Economics and Development.
8 Memorial University Library also reported: Dept of Fisheries (mimeo. and printed) - B; Tourism - no printed annual report; Dept. of Urban & Regional Planning - surveys (no printed reports) - B; Dept. of Housing (printed 1965) - A; All annual reports 1949 - A; Nfld. Royal Commissions 1949 - A; Regional Surveys (Urban and Regional Planning) - A; Nfld. Archives and Museum annual reports - A; Provincial list of electors 1949 - A; Census prior to 1949 - B.

LIBRARY RESOURCES / 87

Queen's Univ. Douglas Lib.[9]	Toronto Public Lib.	Univ. of Toronto Main Lib.[10]	Univ. of Windsor Main Lib.[11]	York Univ. Steacie Sc. Lib.	York University Osgoode Law Sch.	Univ. of Man. Eliz. Dafoe Lib.	Univ. of Sask. Murray Mem. Lib.[12]	Univ. of Sask. Law Lib.	Univ. of Alberta Cameron Lib.	Univ. of Calgary Univ. Lib.	Univ. of BC Main Lib.	Univ. of Victoria McPherson Lib.	Vancouver Public Lib.	Lib. of Parliament	Nat. Lib. of Canada	Harvard Univ. Littauer Lib.	Lib. of Congress
A						D								A			
	D					D								B			
						D								B			
B	D	A	D			D	D	D	C	D	D		C	A	A		A
B		B							D		D	D					
									D				A				
A	D	D	D	D		C	C		B	B	D	C	A	A	A		B
										C		D					
									B		D	D					
		A	D	C		D	D		C	C	D	D	D	A	A		B
C	D		D				D		C	D				A	A		
A	D	A	D	D		C	D		A	C	D	D	C	A	A	D	C
A	C	C	D	D		C	D		A	C	B		A	A	A		B
													D				

9 Queen's University Library also reported: Royal Commission Reports - A; Budget speeches - A; *Gazette* - D.
10 University of Toronto reports statutes almost complete from 1900; all others from 1950 only; *Gazette* - D.
11 University of Windsor Library reports: *Gazette* - D; Social Welfare - D.
12 University of Saskatchewan reports: Insurance - D.
*Data not collected.

Newfoundland

The two largest collections of Newfoundland documents are located at the Gosling Memorial Library, St John's, and the Centre for Newfoundland Studies in the Library of Memorial University of Newfoundland. In 1935, at the beginning of the Commission Government period, the Gosling Library received much of the disbanded collection of the Legislative Library and for many years it remained the only library in the province collecting Newfoundlandia. The University Library possessed virtually no Newfoundland documents until 1964 when it acquired two large collections. The present Legislative Library has been collecting Newfoundland documents since it was organized in 1949; the Newfoundland Archives, since 1960. Users rated Memorial University Library as good; Gosling Memorial Library, excellent; the Legislative Library, fair, and the Archives, poor. Gosling Memorial Library did not complete the table of holdings on the questionnaire.

Prince Edward Island

The only collection of any size on the Island is that of the Legislative Library. It received a poor rating from users and was judged badly organized. This assessment may reflect also the small production record of the government, as much as or more than weakness of the collection. St Dunstan's University reported a collection in a telephone interview, but did not return the questionnaire. Amongst extra-provincial university libraries, Queen's University reports the strongest collection of Prince Edward Island documents.

TABLE 7:2

HOLDINGS OF PRINCE EDWARD ISLAND PUBLICATIONS

	Mem. Univ. of Nfld.	Dalhousie Univ. MacDonald Mem. Lib.	Dalhousie Univ. Sir J. Dunn Law	PEI Leg. Lib.	Univ. of NB H. Irving Lib.	McGill Univ. McLennan Lib.	Sir G. Williams University	Univ. de Montréal Main Lib.	Laurentian Univ. Laurentian Lib.	McMaster Univ. Mills Mem. Lib.	Queen's Univ. Douglas Lib.[1]
Debates				A	D	C		D	D		A
Journals		B		A	C	C		D	D	C	A
Sessional papers											
Statutes			B	A	D	C		D			C
Departmental annual reports:											
Agriculture		D		A	D	C			D		A
Education	D	A		A	D	D			D		A
Attorney-General											
Highways				A	D	B			D		A
Labour	D			A	D	B					A
Lands and Forests						B					
Mining											
Municipal Affairs				A							
Provincial Secretary											
Public Accounts		A		*	D	C		C		D	A
Public Health and Welfare				A	D	B	D	C	D		A
Trade and Industry	D			A		B					A

1 Queen's University Library also reported: Royal Commission Reports - A; Budget speeches - B; *Gazette* - D.
2 University of Toronto reports: *Gazette* - D.
3 University of Windsor reports: *Gazette* - D; public welfare - A.
*Data not collected.

LIBRARY RESOURCES / 91

Toronto Public Lib.	Univ. of Toronto Main Lib.[2]	Univ. of Windsor Main Lib.[3]	Waterloo Luth. Univ. (M. Lib.)	York Univ. Steacie Sc. Lib.	York Univ. Osgoode Law Sch.	Univ. of Man. Eliz. Dafoe Lib.	Univ. of Sask. Murray Mem. Lib.	Univ. of Sask. Law Lib.	Univ. of Alberta Cameron Lib.	Univ. of Calgary Univ. Lib.	Univ. of BC Main Lib.	Univ. of Victoria McPherson Lib.	Vancouver Public Lib.	Library of Parliament	National Lib. of Canada	Harvard Univ. Littauer Lib.	Library of Congress
	C			D		D	D		C	D			A			D	
D	D		C	D		D	C		C	C		D	A	A		C	
D						D			D				B				
C	B	D		D		D		D	B	D	B		A	A			A
D	B	D	C			C	D		A	C	B		D	A	A		B
D	C	D	D			C	C		A	B	B	D	D	A	A		A
D		D		D		C	D		C	C	C		D	A	A	D	B
D	C					D	D						A				D
D							C		D								
									C	D	C						
D	B	D				D	C		B	C	A		C	A	A	C	
D		D				B	D		C	C	D		D	A			C
D							D		C	C			D	A			C

TABLE 7:3

HOLDINGS OF NOVA SCOTIA PUBLICATIONS	Mem. Univ. of Nfld.	NS Legislative Lib.	NS Provincial Archives	Dalhousie Univ. MacDonald Mem. Lib.	Dalhousie Univ. Sir. J. Dunn Law Lib.	St. F. X. Univ. Angus MacDonald Lib.	Univ. of NB H. Irving Lib.	McGill Univ. McLennan Lib.	Sir. G. Williams Univ.	Univ. de Montréal Main Lib.	Brock Univ. Main Lib.	Lakehead Univ. Main Lib.	Laurentian Univ. Laurentian Lib.	McMaster Univ. Mills Mem. Lib.[2]
Debates		A	A	B	D	A		D						
Journals		A	A	A			A	B	B				D	C
Sessional papers		A	A				A							
Statutes		A	A		B	A	D	C					D	
Departmental annual reports:														
Agriculture		A	A	B			C	D	D			D		
Attorney-General		A	A											
Education	D	A	A	B			A	C	B		D		D	
Highways		A	A				C	D	D			D		
Labour		A	A				B	D	D			D		
Lands and Forests	D	A	A	B			C	D	D				D	
Mining	D	A	A				B	C			D	D		D	A
Municipal Affairs		A	A				C	D	C					
Provincial Secretary		A	A				C		D					
Public Accounts		A	A	B			C	D	D		D			
Public Health and Welfare		A	A	A			B	D	C	D	D			
Trade and Industry	D	A	A	C			C	D	C					

1 Queen's University Library also reported: Royal Commission Reports - A; Budget speeches - B; *Gazette* - C.
2 McMaster University Library also reported: Power Commission - C.
3 University of Toronto Library reported: *Gazette* - D.
4 University of Windsor reports: public welfare - D.
5 University of Saskatchewan: Fisheries - D.
6 Waterloo Lutheran University reports: Archives - B.

Queen's Univ. Douglas Lib.[1]	Toronto Public Lib.	Univ. of Toronto Main Lib.[3]	Univ. of Windsor Main Lib.[4]	Waterloo Luth. Univ.[6]	York Univ. Steacie Sc. Lib.	York University Osgoode Law Sch.	Univ. of Man. Eliz. Dafoe Lib.	Univ. of Sask. Murray Mem. Lib.[5]	Univ. of Sask. Law Lib.	Univ. of Alberta Cameron Lib.	Univ. of Calgary Univ. Lib.	Simon Fraser Univ. Main Lib.	Univ. of BC Main Lib.	Univ. of Victoria McPherson Lib.	Vancouver Public Lib.	Lib. of Parliament	National Lib. of Canada	Harvard Univ. Littauer Lib.	Lib. of Congress
	D	C					D	D		D			C			A		D	
A	C	C	D		D		D	D		D			B			A		B	
	C						D			D						B			
A	C	B	D				D	D	B	C	D		A	C		A		D	C
B	C	C	D		D		C	C		C	D	D	C		D	A	A		B
	C							C			D								
B	C	B	D		D		C	B		B	C	D	A	C	D	A	A		
B	C	A	A		D		D	D		C	C	D	B		D	A	B		B
	C	B	C		D				D	C	B	D	C		D	A	A		B
	C	B	D		D		D	D		C	D	D	A		D		A		A
	C	A	D		D		B	C		B	D	D	A		D	A	B	D	A
B	C	D	C		D		D	D		C	D	D	A	A		A		B	A
A	C		D		D		D	D		C	D	D	D			A		D	C
A	C	C	D		D		B	C		C	C	D	A		C	A	C		A
B	C	C	D	D	D		B	D		C	B	D	C		D	A	A		A
B	C	A			D		B	D		C	C	D	B		D	A	A		D

Nova Scotia

Although the Legislative Library and the Library of the Public Archives of Nova Scotia report strong holdings of serial publications, the province's libraries received generally low ratings by users. Collections at Saint Francis Xavier, Acadia, and Dalhousie universities were rated as fair, although one user commented that the Dalhousie collection might rate as "good" if it were organized. The Legislative and Archives libraries were generally considered to be "good." The best collection of Nova Scotia documents in an out-of-province university library appears to be located at the University of British Columbia.

New Brunswick

The University of New Brunswick Library reported that since the early 1960s it has attempted to build a comprehensive collection of Maritime documents and to maintain a supplementary collection of annual reports and royal commission reports from other provinces. At the moment, however, users describe the collection as "fair" to "poor," because of few acquisitions in the previous fifty-year period. Mount Allison's is considered to be poor. The ratings gave the Legislative Library top place with "good" to "fair." Some libraries of government departments were considered "good," others "poor." The New Brunswick Provincial Archives plans to establish a book collection to support its collection of primary materials. However, it has been established too recently to have made much progress in this direction.

The comment of one user summarizes the situation in the province: "None of the libraries has a basic collection of documents. They are scattered through the departments of government, the Legislative Library, and the university libraries."

Queen's and the University of British Columbia possess the strongest collections of New Brunswick documents amongst out-of-province university libraries.

TABLE 7:4

HOLDINGS OF NEW BRUNSWICK PUBLICATIONS	Mem. Univ. of Nfld.	Dalhousie Univ. MacDonald Mem. Lib.	Dalhousie Univ. Sir J. Dunn Law Lib.	NB Legislative Lib.	Univ. of NB H. Irving Lib.[4]	McGill Univ. McLennan Lib.	Sir G. Williams Univ.	Univ. de Montréal Main Lib.	Brock Univ. Main Lib.	Lakehead Univ. Main Lib.	Laurentian Univ. Laurentian Lib.	McMaster Univ. Mills Mem. Lib.
Debates					A	D	D					
Journals			B		A	A	C					
Sessional papers												
Statutes			B		A	A	B	D			D	D
Departmental annual reports:												
Agriculture					A	A	D	D				
Attorney-General					A							
Education		D	A		A	A	C	D				D
Highways					A	B	D					
Labour		D	C		A	A						
Lands and Forests			D		A	B	C			D		
Mining					A	B	C		D			D
Municipal Affairs		D			A	B	D					
Provincial Secretary					A	A	D					
Public Accounts		D	B		*	B	D	D				D
Public Health and Welfare					A	A	D	D	D			
Trade and Industry		D			A	A	D					

1 Queen's University Library also reports: Royal Commission Reports - A; Budget speeches - B; *Gazette* - C.
2 University of Manitoba Library also reports: Dept. of Fisheries - A; Dept. of Youth and Welfare - B.
3 University of British Columbia, Main Library, reports: Dept. of Municipal Affairs 1954; Dept. of Provincial Secretary 1963.
4 University of New Brunswick reports that it is strongest in holdings of geological surveys "although far from complete."
5 University of Toronto Library reports: *Gazette* - D.
6 University of Windsor reports: Youth and Welfare - A.
7 University of Saskatchewan reports: Insurance - D; Fisheries - D.
*Data not collected.

	Queen's Univ. Douglas Lib.[1]	Toronto Public Lib.	Univ. of Toronto Main Lib.[5]	Univ. of Windsor Main Lib.[6]	Waterloo Luth. Lib.	York Univ. Steacie Sc. Lib.	York Univ. Osgoode Law Sch.	Univ. of Man. Eliz. Dafoe Lib.[2]	Univ. of Sask. Murray Mem. Lib.[7]	Univ. of Sask. Law Lib.	Univ. of Alberta Cameron Lib.	Univ. of Calgary Univ. Lib.	Univ. of BC Main Lib.[3]	Univ. of Victoria McPherson Lib.	Vancouver Public Lib.	Lib. of Parliament	National Lib. of Canada	Harvard Univ. Littauer Lib.	Lib. of Congress
			A					D	B			D	A		D	A			
	A	C	C	D	B		D	D	B			D	A	C	D	A	A	C	D
		C						D				D				B	B		
	A	C	A	C			D	D	D	C	B	D	B		D	A	A	D	C
	A	C	B	D			D		C	C	B	C	A		D	A	A		
						D			D	D	D								
	A	C	B	D			D		C	B	C	C	A	D	D	A	A		A
									D		D								
	B	C	A			D		B	B		C	C	A		D	A	A		C
	A	D	C	D		B		C	D		C	D	A		D	A	A		A
	A	D	C			B		C	D			D	A		D	A			
	B	C	D	D	D	D		C	C		C	D		B	D	A	C	C	A
		D		A		D		D	C			D				A			A
	A	C	A		C	D		D	C		C	D	A		C	A	A	D	
	A	B	B	D	D	D		C	D		B	D	A		C	A			B
			C						D				A		D	A	A		A

TABLE 7:5

HOLDINGS OF QUEBEC PUBLICATIONS	Mem. Univ. of Nfld.	Dalhousie Univ. MacDonald Lib.	Dalhousie Univ. Sir J. Dunn Law Lib.	Univ. of NB H. Irving Lib.	Quebec Legis. Lib.	McGill Univ. McLennan Lib.	Sir G. Williams Univ.[5]	Univ. de Montréal Main Lib.[6]	Univ. de Sherbrooke, Main Lib.	Brock Univ. Main Lib.	Lakehead Univ. Main Lib.	Laurentian Univ. Laurentian Lib.	McMaster Univ. Mills Mem. Lib.[3]
Debates	D					A	C	D	B	A		B	
Journals		B				A	A	C	A	A		B	
Sessional papers						A	A	C		A			D
Statutes			B	D		A	A	B	A	A		B	B
Departmental annual reports:													
Agriculture		D			D	A	D	D	B	B		C	
Attorney-General						A			B			D	
Education	D	A			C	A	B	D	A	B		C	B
Highways		D			D	A	C	D	A	B		D	
Labour		D				A	C	D	A	B		D	
Lands and Forests					D	A	C	D	B	B	D	D	
Mining					C	A.	C	D	D	B		D	C	A
Municipal Affairs						A	D			B		D	
Provincial Secretary		D				A		D	D	B			
Public Accounts		B			D	*	C	D	A	B			
Public Health and Welfare		D			D	A	A	D	A	B			
Trade and Industry					D	A	D	D	D	B			

1 Queen's University Library also reports: Royal Commission reports - A; Budget speeches - A; *Gazette* - C.
2 University of British Columbia, Main Library, reports Sessional Papers 1876 - 1903; 1919-36.
3 McMaster University Library also reports: Archives - B; Streams Commission - B.
4 University of Toronto Library reports: Journals Leg. Assembly 1871-1922; Journals Leg. Assembly 1889-1919; Sessional Papers 1869-1919; *Gazette* - D.
5 Sir George Williams University Library reports: Bureau of Statistics - C.
6 University of Montreal reports: Fisheries - D; Finances - C; Natural Resources - D.
7 University of Saskatchewan reports: Fisheries - D.
8 Waterloo Lutheran University reports: Archives - B.
*Data not collected.

LIBRARY RESOURCES / 99

Queen's Univ. Douglas Lib.[1]	Toronto Public Lib.	Univ. of Toronto Main Lib.[4]	Univ. of Windsor Main Lib.	Waterloo Luth. Univ.[8]	York Univ. Steacie Sc. Lib.	York Univ. Osgoode Law Sch.	Univ. of Manitoba Eliz. Dafoe Lib.	Univ. of Sask. Murray Mem. Lib.[7]	Univ. of Sask. Law Lib.	Univ. of Alberta Cameron Lib.	Univ. of Calgary Univ. Lib.	Simon Fraser Univ. Main Lib.	Univ. of BC Main Lib.[2]	Univ. of Victoria McPherson Lib.	Vancouver Public Lib.	Lib. of Parliament	National Lib. of Canada	Harvard Univ. Littauer Lib.	Lib. of Congress
A			A	D		D		D			D		A		A			D	D
A	C		C	D		D		D			D		A		A			C	B
A	C		D	D		D		C							B			C	
A	A	B	D		A		D	C		B	B	A	A	D	D	A	B	D	B
B	C	B	D		D		C	D		C	D		B		A				B
								D			D								
A	D	C	D		D		B	C		C	C	A	A	D	D	A			C
A	C	D	D	D	D			D		C	C				D	A			C
		C	C		C		D	D	D	D		A		D	D	A			D
A	C	A	D	D	B			D			D		A	A	D	A			C
A	D	D			C		C	D		C	D		B		D	A			D
B			D		D			D		C	D		C	C	D	A			C
					D										A				
A	C	C	D		D		C	C		C	C		A		C	A		D	D
A	D		C		D		D	D		D	D		A		D	A			D
B	D	D			D			D		D	D		D		D	A			C

Quebec

According to one user, the best collections of Quebec documents in the province are in the Legislative Library (Quebec), Ecole des Hautes Etudes Commerciales (Montreal), and Bibliothèque Nationale (Montreal). The Provincial Archives and the Montreal Public Library have collections that were considered extremely good by others, but neither returned the questionnaire. Those of the universities of McGill, Laval, Sherbrooke, and Montreal were described as "good," although one user reported that Laval has only a partial collection. Laval did not respond to the questionnaire.

Only the Legislative Library, the Libraries of Montreal and McGill Universities, and the Bibliothèque Nationale appear to be collecting documents of other provinces. The Legislative Library does not claim to have a complete set of publications from other provinces. McGill's Redpath Library reported attempting to acquire journals, gazettes, statutes, annual reports, and royal commissions from all provinces and anything else which appears "a worthwhile study in some depth." The University of Montreal is only interested in other provinces' statutes, public accounts, and debates. The Bibliothèque Nationale has a highly selective approach to the publications of other provinces.

Ontario

Users found the Legislative Library "good" to "excellent," although more than one noted that many documents are not in the collection. Historians found the Provincial Archives' Library also "good" to "excellent"; political scientists and economists described it as "fair" to "poor." A group of librarians reported that they could not locate items listed in the Archives' catalogue. The Archives points out that the collection is maintained only as a support to its collection of primary documents and thus no attempt is made to ensure comprehensiveness. One person noted that Ontario Hydro has superb archives, another that the Canadian Tax Foundation has a good library of provincial materials.

Ontario university libraries, for the most part, came under heavy fire. One man was moved to say of the University of Toronto collection: "Badly catalogued and poorly shelved; the whole section is a disgrace." Others were not as passionate, but tended to agree, although one rated it as good and another as good to fair. Queen's was described as good; McMaster and Western, fair (the latter is collecting Ontario documents primarily); Guelph and Waterloo Lutheran, fair to poor; and Waterloo and Carleton, poor. York was rated both good and very poor.

Ontario documents have received probably the broadest circulation and most university libraries report some elements of strength. Again, however, the University of British Columbia collection appears to be the strongest in a university collection outside the province.

102 / GOVERNMENT PUBLISHING IN THE CANADIAN PROVINCES

TABLE 7:6

HOLDINGS OF ONTARIO PUBLICATIONS

	Mem. Univ. of Nfld.	Dalhousie Univ. MacDonald Lib.	Dalhousie Univ. Sir J. Dunn Law Lib.	Univ. of NB H. Irving Lib.	McGill Univ. McLennan Lib.	Sir G. Williams Univ.	Univ. de Montréal Main Lib.	Univ. de Sherbrooke Main Lib.	Ontario Legis. Lib.	Ontario Archives	Brock Univ. Main Lib.	Lakehead Univ. Main Library	Laurentian Univ. Laurentian Lib.	McMaster Univ. Mills Mem. Lib.[2]
Debates	D				C			D	A	A	C	D	B	A
Journals				C	A			D	A	A	C	C	B	A
Sessional papers		D			A			D	A	A	C	D	B	A
Statutes			B	C	A		B	D	A	A	A	A	B	A
Departmental annual reports:														
Agriculture	D	B		D	B		D		A	A	C	C	C	A
Attorney-General	D													
Education				C	A		D	D	A	A	C	C	C	A
Highways	D			D	D			D	A	A	D		C	C
Labour	D	D		C	C	C		D	A	A	D	D	C	C
Lands and Forests	D			D	D		D	D	A	A	D	B	C	C
Mining					A		A	D	A		B	B	C	A
Municipal Affairs				D	D			D	B	A	D	D		A
Provincial Secretary									D	A		D		
Public Accounts				C			A	D	*	*	D	A		C
Public Health and Welfare	D	D		C	D	D	D	D	A	A	D		C	B
Trade and Industry					D			D	A		D	D		

1 Queen's University Library also reports: Royal Commission Reports - A; Budget speeches - A; *Gazette* - B.
2 McMaster University Library also reports: Hydro-Electric Power Commission - B; Vital Statistics-Registrar General - C; Workmens Compensation - C; Archives - A.
3 University of Toronto Library reports: *Gazette* - D.
4 University of Windsor reports: *Gazette* - D; Public Welfare - D.
5 Waterloo Lutheran University reports: Hydro-Electric Power Commission - B; Civil Service Commission - D.
*Data not collected.

LIBRARY RESOURCES / 103

	Queen's Univ. Douglas Lib.[1]	Toronto Public Lib.	Trent Univ. Main Lib.	Univ. of Toronto Main Lib.[3]	Univ. of Windsor Main Lib.[4]	Waterloo Luth. Univ.[5]	York University Steacie Sc. Lib.	Univ. of Manitoba Eliz. Dafoe Lib.	Univ. of Sask. Murray Mem. Lib.	Univ. of Sask. Law Lib.	Univ. of Alberta Cameron Lib.	Univ. of Calgary Univ. Lib.	Simon Fraser Univ.	Univ. of BC Main Lib.	Univ. of Victoria McPherson Lib.	Vancouver Public Lib.	Lib. of Parliament	National Lib. of Canada	Harvard Univ. Littauer Lib.	Lib. of Congress
	A	A		A	D	D	A	C	D			D		C			A	D		D
	A	A		A	D	A	A		D			D		A	C	D	A	B	C	B
	A	A		A	D	A	A		B			D	A	A			B	C	B	D
	A	A	C	A	A	A	A	C	B	B	C	C	A	D	C	D	A	B		C
	A	A		A	D	D	B	B	B		C	D		C		D	A	C	C	B
								D					D	A		C	A	C		C
	A	A	B	A	D	C	B	D	C		B	D	D	B	D	D	A	A		B
	A	B		B	C	D	C	D	D		C	C		A						
	A	A		C		D	C	C	D		C	D		A	D	C	A	A		A
	A	A	C	B	B	C	A	D	D		C	D		A	D	D	A	A	D	B
	A	A		A	B	A	A	B	C		B	A	D	A	D	D	A	A	D	B
	A	A		A	D	C	D	D	D		C	C	D	A	C		A	D	D	A
							D													
	A	A		C	D	D	C	C	C		C	C	D	A	D	C	A	D	D	B
	A	A		C	C	B	C	B	C		C	D		A		C	A	A	D	B
	A						D	D			D	D				D				C

104 / GOVERNMENT PUBLISHING IN THE CANADIAN PROVINCES

TABLE 7:7

HOLDINGS OF MANITOBA PUBLICATIONS	Mem. Univ. of Nfld.	Dalhousie Univ. MacDonald Mem. Lib.	Dalhousie Univ. Sir J. Dunn Law. Lib.	Univ. of NB H. Irving Lib.	McGill Univ. McLennan Lib.	Sir G. Williams Univ. Main Lib.	Univ. de Montréal Main Lib.	Brock Univ. Main Lib.	Lakehead Univ. Main Library	Laurentian Univ. Laurentian Lib.	McMaster Univ. Mills Mem. Lib.	Queen's Univ. Douglas Lib.[1]
Debates		D								D		A
Journals		B		D	C		D		D	D		A
Sessional papers				D							D	A
Statutes			B	C	C		D		D	D	D	A
Departmental annual reports:												
Agriculture					D							A
Attorney-General												
Education	D	A		C	A	D	D		D	D	C	A
Highways					A							B
Labour		D		D	B		D			D		A
Lands and Forests					B			D				A
Mining				C	B		D		C		A	A
Municipal Affairs	D				D							B
Provincial Secretary												
Public Accounts		A		D			C					A
Public Health and Welfare		D		D	D	D	D					A
Trade and Industry	D				B							

1 Queen's University Library also reports: Royal Commission Reports - A; Budget speeches - A; *Gazette* - C.
2 University of British Columbia, main library reports: Debates: 1963; Dept. of Agriculture reports: 1960.
3 University of Toronto reports: *Gazette* - D.
4 University of Windsor reports: *Gazette* - D.
5 University of Saskatchewan reports: Co-operation - D; Insurance - D.
*Data not collected.

LIBRARY RESOURCES / 105

Toronto Public Lib.	Univ. of Toronto Main Lib.[3]	Univ. of Windsor Main Lib.[4]	Waterloo Lutheran Univ.	York Univ. Steacie Sc. Lib.	Manitoba Legis. Lib.	Univ. of Manitoba Eliz. Dafoe Lib.	Univ. of Sask. Murray Mem. Lib.[5]	Univ. of Sask. Law Lib.	Univ. of Alberta Cameron Lib.	Univ. of Calgary University Lib.	Univ. of BC Main Lib.[2]	Univ. of Victoria McPherson Lib.	Vancouver Public Lib.	Lib. of Parliament	National Lib. of Canada.	Harvard Univ. Littauer Library	Lib. of Congress
	A			D	A	B	D		C	D				A	B		D
A	C		D	D	A	B	C		C	D	A	D	D	A	A		B
C	C			D	A	B	D			D	A			B	B		
B	A	D		D	A	A	C	A	B	D	A		D	A	A		B
D	D	D		D	A	A/D	D		C	D	D	D	D	A	B		C
C	A	D		B	A	B	D		A	D	A	C	D	A	A		A
		D		B	A	D			D	D	A		D	A	A		D
C	C	D		D	A	C	A		C	D	A	D		A	A		A
					A	C						D	D				A
B	C	D	D	C	A	B	D		C	D	A	D	D	A	A		A
	C	D			D/A	D/B	D		C	D	A	A	D	A	A		A
C	B	D		C	*	B	C		C	D		D	C	A	A	C	A
B	B	D			D	A	B	D		C	D	A	D	C	A	A	A
B	A				A	B	D		C	D	A	C	D	A	A		A

Manitoba

Users found that the Manitoba Legislative Library has the best collection of provincial documents within the province. It was described as "good" to "fair" while the University of Manitoba was considered "fair." The University of British Columbia and Queen's University possess stronger collections of Manitoba documents than any other universities outside the province.

Saskatchewan

Again, the Legislative Library's collection of documents received top rating. It was described as good to excellent and well catalogued. Opinions of the Archives and the University of Saskatchewan collection at Saskatoon varied, perhaps according to the researcher's needs. Descriptions of the Archives ranged from "good" to "fair"; those of the University ranged from "good" to "poor." Some commented that cataloguing of the latter collection and staff assistance in locating material could be improved. The latter was reported to be trying to obtain from all provinces annual reports, other sessional papers, and departmental publications in which researchers on campus were particularly interested. The collection at the Regina campus is too new and too close to the Legislative Library to have achieved any sizable holdings of provincial publications. Queen's, the University of Toronto, the University of British Columbia, and the Toronto Public Library all report good collections of Saskatchewan publications.

TABLE 7:8

HOLDINGS OF SASKATCHEWAN PUBLICATIONS	Mem. Univ. of Nfld.	Dalhousie Univ. MacDonald Mem. Lib.	Dalhousie Univ. Sir J. Dunn Law Lib.	Univ. of NB H. Irving Lib.	McGill Univ. McLennan Lib.	Sir G. Williams Univ.	Univ. de Montréal	Brock Univ.	Laurentian Univ. Laurentian Lib.	McMaster Univ. Mills Mem. Lib.	Queen's Univ. Douglas Lib.[1]	Toronto Public Lib.
Debates	D			D	B	D			D	D	A	D
Journals					B	A					A	A
Sessional papers					D	C					A	D
Statutes			B	C			C		D	D	A	A
Departmental annual reports:												
Agriculture	D	D			D				D		A	A
Attorney-General												
Education	D	A		C	A	D	C				A	B
Highways				D	C						A	B
Labour	D	D		D	D		D				A	B
Lands and Forests					C						A	
Mining	D			B	A		D	D		C	A	A
Municipal Affairs	D	D			D						A	B
Provincial Secretary				D								
Public Accounts				C			C				A	A
Public Health and Welfare				C	D	D	D				A	A
Trade and Industry	D											A

1 Queen's University Library also reports: Royal Commission Reports - A; Budget speeches - A; *Gazette* - C.
2 University of Manitoba Library also reports: Dept. of Co-operation and Co-operative Development - B.
3 University of British Columbia, Main Library, reports: Debates: 1946; Journals: 1933.
4 University of Toronto reports: *Gazette* - D.
5 University of Windsor reports: Public Welfare - C.
6 University of Saskatchewan reports: Co-operation - A; Insurance - D; Fisheries - D; Social Welfare - A; Public Works - A; Telephones - A.
7 Waterloo Lutheran University reports: Archives - D.
*Data not collected.

LIBRARY RESOURCES / 109

Univ. Of Toronto Main Lib.[4]	Univ. of Windsor Main Lib.[5]	Waterloo Lutheran Univ.[7]	York University Steacie Sc. Lib.	Univ. of Manitoba Eliz. Dafoe Lib.[2]	Saskatchewan Legislative Lib.	Saskatchewan Archives	Univ. of Sask. Murray Mem. Lib.[6]	Univ. of Sask. Law Lib.	Univ. of Alberta Cameron Lib.	Univ. of Calgary Univ. Lib.	Univ. of BC Main Lib.[3]	Univ. of Victoria McPherson Lib.	Vancouver Public Lib.	Lib. of Parliament	National Lib. of Canada	Harvard Univ. Littauer Lib.	Lib. of Congress
A	D		D	D	A	A	A			C	D			A	A		C
A			D	D	A	A	A		B	D		B	C	A		D	A
A				D	A	A	A							B	B	D	
A	A		D	D	A	A	A	A	B	C	A	B		A	C		B
A	D		B	B	A	A	A		B	D	A	D	B	A	A		A
				A													
A	D		C	D	A	A	A		C	B	A	B	C	A	A		B
A	C		D	D	A	A	A		C	C	A	B	C	A	A		A
A	B	C	D	B	A	A	A		C	C	A	C	C	A	A		A
			B			A	B					C	C				
A	A		D	B	A	A	B		B	D		B	D	A	A		A
A	C		B	C	A	A	A		C	D	B	B	C	A	A	A	A
					A	A	A										
A	D		D	A	*	*	A			D	A	C	C	A	A	A	A
C	D		D	B	A	A	A		C	D	A	D	C	A	A		C
A			D		A	A	A			D		B	D	A	A		D

TABLE 7:9

HOLDINGS OF ALBERTA PUBLICATIONS

	Memorial Univ. of Nfld.	Dalhousie Univ. MacDonald Mem. Lib.	Dalhousie Univ. Sir J. Dunn Law Lib.	Univ. of NB H. Irving Lib.	McGill Univ. McLennan Lib.	Sir G. Williams Univ.	Univ. de Montréal Main Library	Brock University	Laurentian Univ. Laurentian Lib.	McMaster Univ. Mills Mem. Lib.	Queen's Univ. Douglas Lib.[1]	Toronto Public Lib.
Debates												
Journals					D	C	D				A	B
Sessional papers												
Statutes			B	D					D	D	A	A
Departmental annual reports:												
Agriculture	D				D	C					A	B
Attorney-General												
Education			A		B	A	C			D	A	A
Highways					D	D					B	C
Labour	D											
Lands and Forests	D				D	D			D	D	B	A
Mining					D	D		D	D	A	B	B
Municipal Affairs					D	D					A	B
Provincial Secretary											A	
Public Accounts			B		D				D	C	A	B
Public Health and Welfare					D		D				A	B
Trade and Industry	D											

1 Queen's University Library also reports: Royal Commission reports - A; Budget speeches - A; *Gazette* - A.
2 University of British Columbia, Main Library, reports: Dept. of Lands and Forests 1949-50; Dept. of Mining 1949.
3 University of Alberta reports: Alberta Research Council - B.
4 University of Toronto reports: *Gazette* - D.
5 University of Windsor reports: *Gazette* - D; Public Welfare - C.
*Data not collected.

LIBRARY RESOURCES / 111

	Univ. of Toronto Main Lib.[4]	Univ. of Windsor Main Lib.[5]	Waterloo Lutheran Univ.	York Univ. Steacie Sc. Lib.	Univ. of Manitoba Eliz. Dafoe Lib.	Univ. of Sask. Murray Mem. Lib.	Univ. of Sask. Law Lib.	Alberta Provincial Lib.	Alberta Provincial Archives	Calgary Public Lib.	Univ. of Alberta Cameron Lib.[3]	Univ. of Calgary Univ. Lib.	Simon Fraser Univ. Main Lib.	Univ. of BC Main Lib.[2]	Univ. of Victoria McPherson Lib.	Vancouver Public Lib.	Lib. of Parliament	National Lib. of Canada	Harvard Univ. Littauer Lib.	Lib. of Congress
1					D						D									
2	A				D	D		A		B	C	D		A		D	A	B	A	A
3					D	D		A									B	C		D
4	A	D			C	A		A	A	A	A	B	B	A	A		C	A	A		B
5	A	D		B	B	A		A	A	A	A	A	D	A		D	A	C		A
6	A	D		D	B	A		A	C	A	A	A		A	D	A	A	A		A
7	A	D		D		D		A	A	A	A	D		B		D	A	A		A
8	A	D		C	D	C		A	B	A	B	D			D	D	A	A		C
9	A	B		A	A	C		A	A	A	A	D			D	D	A	A		A
10	C	D	D	D	D	C		A	B	A	B	B	A	D	B	A	A		C	A
11		D			D	D		A	C	B	B	D		D		D	A	B	D	D
12	A	D	D	C	B	B		*	*	A	A	B	D	C	D	C	A	A	A	C
13	B	D	D	D	B	B		A	A	B	A	B		A		C	A	A		B
14	B					D		A				D				D	A	A		D

Alberta

Alberta was another province in which users did not arrive at a consensus in naming the best collection. One person found some gaps in the Provincial Library's holdings but considered it to be an excellent collection, another described it as fair to poor, the remainder ranged between these extremes. The broad variation in the assessment of this particular collection may be due to the fact that Mr E.C. Holmgren, Provincial Librarian, reports sending most specialized material to departments, where he hopes it will receive more use than in his own library. Most users found the collections of the universities of Alberta and Calgary fair and the Glenbow Foundation's collection only fair in general but very good for the early territorial government period. T.R. McCloy, Librarian of the Foundation, reports: "We have a very meagre scattering [of publications] from Saskatchewan and Manitoba, with no runs of any type. For Alberta we do somewhat better. We have a complete run of Department of Agriculture annual reports and all the Statutes up to the 1950s. We also have a good run of the Alberta *Gazette* and a complete set of the old Northwest Territories *Gazette*. We have scattered reports for most Alberta Government Departments but no good runs other than those I have already mentioned" (Letter to A.P. Pross, 24 June 1969). The Calgary Public Library reported that its collection of Alberta documents is particularly strong in information relating to the oil industry.

In the other provinces, good university collections of Alberta documents are maintained by University of British Columbia, University of Toronto, and Queen's University. The Toronto Public Library possesses a collection that outranks those of most university libraries.

British Columbia

British Columbia's Legislative Library was credited with possessing the best collection of the province's documents. Nevertheless, one user commented: "I can usually find a better collection in a government department than in any library. Perhaps the Legislative Library does not catalogue some material. Anyway, it is easier to find in the departments. In other provinces, also, I spend more time in provincial government offices getting information than in the Legislative Library."

Users did not reply in sufficient numbers to permit evaluation of the university collections. The University of British Columbia Library reported that it is not attempting to gather a complete collection from other provinces except in the fields of education, agriculture, forestry, geology, economics, and health. Simon Fraser University's policy is to acquire complete sets of British Columbia and Alberta documents. Royal Roads Military College reported that "lack of space prevents and proximity to the Legislative Library makes unnecessary the maintenance of a provincial government documents collection."

Outside the province the University of Alberta and Queen's University lead all other academic institutions in strength of collection.

114 / GOVERNMENT PUBLISHING IN THE CANADIAN PROVINCES

TABLE 7:10

HOLDINGS OF BRITISH COLUMBIA PUBLICATIONS

	Memorial Univ. of Nfld.	Dalhousie Univ. MacDonald Mem. Lib.	Dalhousie Univ. Sir J. Dunn Law Lib.	Univ. of NB H. Irving Lib.	McGill Univ. McLennan Lib.	Sir G. Williams Univ.	Univ. de Montréal Main Lib.	Brock Univ.	Lakehead Univ. Main Lib.	Laurentian Univ.	McMaster Univ. Mills Mem. Lib.	Queen's Univ. Douglas Lib.[1]
Debates												
Journals		C		D	B							A
Sessional papers		C									D	A
Statutes			B	D	C		D			D	D	A
Departmental annual reports:												
Agriculture		D		D	B							A
Attorney-General		D										
Education		A		D						D		A
Highways					D							B
Labour	D	B		D	A		C					A
Lands and Forests				D			D		C	D	C	A
Mining				D			B	D	D	C	B	A
Municipal Affairs				C	D					D		A
Provincial Secretary		D										
Public Accounts		A		D	D		B				D	A
Public Health and Welfare		D		D		D	C					A
Trade and Industry				D	C							A

1 Queen's University Library also reports: Royal Commission Reports - A; Budget speeches - A; *Gazette* - B.
2 University of Alberta reports: BC Research Council - B.
3 University of Toronto Library reports: *Gazette* - D.
4 University of Windsor reports: Public Welfare - D.
*Data not collected.

LIBRARY RESOURCES / 115

Toronto Public Lib.	Univ. of Toronto Main Lib.[3]	Univ. of Windsor Main Lib.[4]	Waterloo Lutheran Univ.	York Univ. Steacie Sc. Lib.	Univ. of Manitoba Eliz. Dafoe Lib.	Univ. of Sask. Murray Mem. Lib.	Univ. of Sask. Law Lib.	Univ. of Alberta Cameron Lib.[2]	Univ. of Calgary Univ. Lib.	Univ. of BC Provincial Lib.	Simon Fraser Univ. Main Lib.	Univ. of BC Main Lib.	Univ. of Victoria McPherson Lib.	Vancouver Public Lib.	Lib. of Parliament	National Lib. of Canada	Harvard Univ. Littauer Lib.	Lib. of Congress
				D														
B	D	B		D	D	D			A	A	A	C	A	A		C	A	
C	D			D	D	C		D	A		A	D	A	B		B		
C	A	D		C	D	D	A	A	C	A	A	B	A	A	B			
C	B			C	B	C		B	D	A	A	D	A	A	B	D	A	
		B		D		D		B		A	A	A			A		D	
C	C	D		D	C	B		B	C	A	A	B	A	A			B	
A		B		D	C	D		B	D	A	A	A	A	A	A		D	
A	A	D		C	D	D		B	C	A	A	A	A	A	A		A	
A	C			C	B	C		B	C	A	A		A	A	A	D	A	
B	A	D		B	A	D		C	B	A	A	A	A	A	A		A	
A			D	D	C	D		B	D	A	A	B	A	A	A		A	
				D		C		B	D	A	A	A	A				A	
C	C	D		B	B	C		B	D	*	A	A	C	A	A	A	C	A
C	C		D	B	C	C		C	D	A	A	B	A	A			C	
B	A			C	D	D		C	D	A	A	B	A	A	D		A	

HANSARD

In Newfoundland prior to 1909 there was no official Hansard. However, good collections of newspapers for this period are housed in the Gosling Memorial Library and the Newfoundland Archives. Although an official Hansard was begun in 1909, financial problems caused its demise after 1931 and Commission government was set up in 1933. Between 1949 and 1957 it was again published, but not indexed. After 1957, it was kept only in typescript, but on 23 May 1968 the Legislature voted to publish it and to allow debates to be reported in both French and English. It was estimated that the backlog would be published at the rate of two sessions per year. As far as is known, no volumes have appeared.

Formal reports of the debates of Prince Edward Island's Legislature were made between 1851 and 1893, in 1914, 1915, 1924, and 1925. Since 1960, the debates on the Speech from the Throne and the Budget have been published. Present newspaper reports are said to have an editorial slant.

Nova Scotia's debates were first published as a separate document in 1855 and continued until 1916, though lapsing in 1862. In 1951 they resumed. A daily issue has appeared since 1953 but is not available on a mail-order basis. A good collection of newspapers containing reports of earlier debates can be found at the Public Archives of Nova Scotia.

Debates have been published under the title of *Synoptic Reports* for many years in New Brunswick. They began for the session of 1837/38, but appeared only irregularly until 1883. Since 1884 they have appeared annually. Before 1968 they were published at the end of session only; however, for 1968's session a daily Hansard appeared, which the Queen's Printer is satisfied will replace the *Synoptic Reports*. These will not be collected and bound at the end of sessions.

In Quebec, Hansard has been printed in French since 1963 and indexed since 1964. It appears in French only. Committee minutes are included in the last volume. Of historic interest is the work compiled by G. Alphonse Desjardins, *Débats de la Législature provinciale de la Province de Québec, 1879-1892*. However, it is not indexed. The Legislative Library does not have a scrapbook Hansard.

Ontario's Legislative Library has maintained a scrapbook for each session since 1867. A microfilm has been made of those covering the period from 30 December 1867 to 5 April 1946. Each reel is indexed, although its arrangement varies. Official Hansard began in 1946. Even so, the Legislative Library still keeps a scrapbook to serve as a quick index for the current session until the official index has been compiled.

The Provincial Library of Manitoba has kept scrapbooks of newspaper debates since 1885. These include clippings from the *Free Press* and the *Tribune*. Since 1958 the official debates have been published. Each volume is indexed, but not extensively.

The Debates and Proceedings of the Legislative Assembly of Saskatchewan have been published for every year since 1948 except 1949. At the end of each session it is edited, bound, and indexed to some extent. The Legislative Library maintained a newspaper scrapbook from 1888 to 1958 that contains almost verbatim reports of debates. These have not been indexed, although the Legislative Library's Newspaper Index, which covers the period 1935 to 1965, could be used. The Saskatchewan Archives has scrapbooks of newspaper debates, which seem to have been compiled in a ministerial office in Regina between 1906 and 1939, as well as other clippings grouped on topics; however, these sets are not necessarily complete. A guide at the Archives titled *A Listing of the Collection of Newspapers and Newspaper Clippings in the Archives of Saskatchewan,* Saskatoon, 1962, provides some help in approaching this material.

Since 1965, when recording equipment was installed in Alberta's Legislature, the province's debates on the Speech from the Throne and the Budget have been published. Photo-copies of the official transcripts are available at a cost of five cents per page. There is some hope that all debates will be recorded and published eventually. Scrapbooks of newspaper reports go back to 1905, when the province was created. For the early period, newspaper reporting appears to have been extensive and reasonably objective, but recently an editorial bias has become more obvious. The newspaper debates until 1964 are kept by the Legislative Library and are indexed at least from 1910.

There has never been a Hansard in British Columbia. Since 1925 the Legislative Library has indexed each of the two main newspapers in Victoria and Vancouver for provincial material. When the Legislature sits, the Library takes extra copies of these journals and clips and mounts those items referring to the debates. In addition, mimeographed copies of ministerial statements have been circulated from time to time.

ROYAL COMMISSION MATERIALS

Interested libraries experience only moderate difficulty in collecting published reports of royal commissions, since these are usually obtainable from either the provincial Queen's Printer, the department most closely concerned with the subject matter of the report, or from the premier's office. However, transcripts, research material, and submissions have seldom been systematically collected in the past and even today are not always automatically deposited in provincial archives.

The problem arises out of the fact that these supporting documents may be categorized in at least four ways: as government publications, archival documents, official records, or part of a public figure's personal files. Different actors have variously interpreted their responsibilities towards these materials, with the result that until recently no one repository has been singled out to house them. Submissions are often obtainable only from the individuals or groups presenting them; libraries often find that extra copies are not available. One academic was refused a copy of a publicly presented brief on the grounds that it was a confidential document. Again, while the commissioners themselves frequently keep personal copies of major briefs, research reports, and transcripts, they are not always willing to part with them. Libraries may negotiate for many years for such documents, only to see them destroyed by fire or by an uninterested heir.

Good arrangements for the care of royal commission records exist in British Columbia. The report, transcripts, anything filed with the commission, and anything the commission may on its own acquire must be filed with the Provincial Secretary who has the Provincial Library and Archives in his department. At present, the material cannot be serviced due to a shortage of staff, but its preservation is assured and there is a possibility of improvement in the future.

In the absence of such arrangements, libraries in other provinces must in most cases content themselves with the printed reports of commissions, and, if their aim is good research collection, the materials that can be gathered up through applications to commissioners and authors of submissions. Legislative libraries, Archives, and the National Library of Quebec are the most likely places to find these. Some university libraries (e.g., Dalhousie, University of Toronto, University of Manitoba, University of British Columbia) also try to collect them. However, no library of any type has been completely successful in its endeavours.

ELECTION DATA

A supplementary questionnaire asked libraries responding to the initial enquiry to provide information concerning their holdings of reports of the chief returning officers for the provinces, instructions to returning officers, and electoral maps. The response, while quite incomplete, has been sufficiently detailed to preclude adequate analysis here. It is hoped that the analysis will be published in an appropriate academic journal when it has been completed. In the meantime, the following paragraphs are intended to provide a general indication of the state of library holdings in this field.

Several provinces require, or have in the past required, that election returns be reported officially as part of the sessional papers or in the provincial *Gazette*. These include Newfoundland, where they are usually published in the *Gazette* about four weeks after the returns are tabulated; New Brunswick, in the *Journal of the Legislative Assembly* until 1967 when the Chief Electoral Officer began publishing a separate report; and Ontario, in the *Sessional Papers* from 1867-1948. In Nova Scotia election reports are tabled in the Assembly and the Legislative Library maintains a very complete record, presumably based on these returns.

Ontario data are also available in Roderick A. Lewis, *A History of the Electoral Districts, Legislatures and Ministries of the Province of Ontario, 1867-1968* (Toronto: Queen's Printer, 1968), while the Legislative Library, the Toronto Public Library, Waterloo University Library, and the University of Toronto have significant collections of returns and other documents.

The documents issued by the chief returning officers of Alberta are still in the hands of the Clerk of the Legislature, but the University of Alberta, Cameron Library, has a strong collection of returns and the Provincial Archives possesses a number of maps and returns for a few years.

In British Columbia the Provincial Library has strong holdings of maps, instructions, and returns, while other significant collections are maintained by Waterloo University Library, the Library of Parliament, and the Vancouver Public Library. Similarly, in Quebec significant collections are reported by the Library of the National Assembly, the University of Montreal, McGill, the Library of Parliament, Waterloo University, Sherbrooke University, and University of Toronto.

Data for Saskatchewan, Manitoba, and Prince Edward Island are most elusive, since these provinces apparently neither publish official returns nor ensure that official records are deposited in any more than one centre other than the office of the chief electoral officer. In Saskatchewan and Manitoba the legislative libraries hold some records, those of the Manitoba Provincial Library probably being the more complete, but in Prince Edward Island only the Chief Electoral Officer maintains adequate records.

Professor T.H. Qualter, of the University of Waterloo, appears to possess the country's only comprehensive collection of documents relating to provincial electoral law, library collections of instructions to returning officers and similar materials being extremely thin.

PUBLICATIONS ON MICROFILM

Some provincial government publications are available on microfilm. The Photographic Service Division of the New York Public Library sells microfilms of partial runs of all provinces' gazettes.* In addition, Simon Fraser University Library reported plans to microfilm the *British Columbia Gazette.* Ontario's newspaper Hansard from 30 December 1867, to 5 April 1946 has been filmed in fourteen indexed reels. The Archives of Manitoba has been filming everything tabled in the Legislature. The papers, dating back to 1870, will be organized on a

---

*Available are: *Newfoundland Gazette*, 1955-65; Prince Edward Island, *Royal Gazette*, 1957-66, Incomplete. Nova Scotia, *Royal Gazette*, 1949-65, Incomplete. New Brunswick, *Royal Gazette*, 1957-64; Quebec, *Gazette Officiel*, 1953-66; *Ontario Gazette*, 1958-65; *Manitoba Gazette*, 1957-66; *Saskatchewan Gazette*, 1958-66; *Alberta Gazette*, 1951-65; *British Columbia Gazette*, 1957-66.

sessional basis with table of contents and subject index. The projected completion date was August 1969. These films will be available on interlibrary loan.

Most librarians and archivists interviewed were interested in microfilming as a means of cutting purchasing and storage costs, as well as acquiring unpublished material. Some libraries possessing microfilming facilities were willing to co-operate in filming should a general project be set afoot. Most were willing to have materials in their libraries microfilmed, but did not wish rare items to leave the confines of the library itself. A travelling microfilm unit could meet this restriction. The libraries that had no microfilm readers and saw no merit in a microfilm project were decidedly in a minority; almost all expressed interest in obtaining the product of a microfilming project.

When asked to suggest priorities in microfilming, respondents differed. Many thought Royal Commission papers should be put on film first. Some suggested records of legislative committees; others newspaper Hansards. Some felt that annual reports should receive first priority, although others found these more readily available than the other material.

ACCESS

The collections described in this chapter are accessible to users under varying conditions.

Legislative libraries serve legislatures first. Most allow the public to use their collections on the premises, but lending items to people who are not MLAs or civil servants for use outside the library is not common practice, especially when a legislature is in session. The libraries are usually open only from 9.00 to 5.00 Monday to Friday and closed on weekends. Some do not have copying equipment.

A few of the legislative libraries are more stringent in their terms. In Prince Edward Island the member of the public must convince the legislative librarian that he is engaged in a reasonable piece of research. In Ontario he must provide proof that the material he wants cannot be found elsewhere. In British Columbia users stated that while access to the legislative library is made as easy as possible for university faculty members, students require passes that must be renewed on every visit.

Provincial archives' collections are available to the public for use on the premises. Hours are again often inconvenient for users located in distant centres or unable to leave their place of work.

University libraries and public libraries are open longer. Their collections are frequently available to users outside the immediate publics they serve if used in the library.

The government documents of few libraries are available on interlibrary loan. In part this is because they are often not catalogued and consequently do not appear in the National Library's union catalogue. Another reason is that few libraries are willing to lend these documents. One library that both catalogues them and allows them to go out on interlibrary loan - the Toronto Public Library - reports that most dealings in this respect are with university libraries. The National Library lends its own provincial government publications, frail, rare, and oversize items excepted.

GENERAL COMMENTS AND CONCLUSION

The data in this chapter suggest that haphazard and sporadic acquisition of provincial publications has taken place in most university libraries. Only one or two libraries have applied a consistent development policy for any length of time. The result is a combination of scarcity and redundancy; collections in neighbouring institutions show identical strengths and weaknesses. Too many university libraries expect legislative libraries to make up for their deficiencies. The legislative, administrative, and academic communities will demand more and more of the legislative library's facilities and the time may soon come when legislative librarians will have to decide that the academic community must go elsewhere for assistance. This, in effect, is the policy of the Ontario Legislative Library.

The researcher faces even greater difficulties than the failure of the university libraries to apply consistent acquisition policies. Unless he, or the librarian, has personal knowledge of a more complete collection in another library, the investigator has no finding facilities available to him. Location information is lacking in bibliographies and, although the National Library enters provincial documents in its union catalogue, the fact that many libraries do not catalogue or report their own holdings in this field renders the National Catalogue far less useful than it might be, so that interlibrary loan presents only limited possibilities. Furthermore, few libraries circulate these materials on interlibrary loan. The user must travel to other libraries and make arrangements to stay near them while he carries out his research. If he cannot arrange to do this during the course of a normal work week, the doors of most archives and legislative libraries are shut to him, the National Library's 24-hour service again providing a notable exception.

At the same time, there is much waste. Not knowing where else to find his research material, or effectively denied access to it, the researcher persuades his own university library to fit its purchasing policy to his needs. Collections grow at random, reflecting the fads and fancies of the academic world and the needs of faculty members whose stay in the university may be shorter than that of the average undergraduate. In all, the very few resources available in the provincial government publications field are being under-utilized and over-duplicated through lack of co-operation.

Beyond attempting to meet the immediate needs of the researcher, university libraries have done very little to overcome the difficulties we have described. There has been no attempt to rationalize resources - beyond referring inquiries to archive and legislative libraries, a questionable procedure at best. There has been little effort to create adequate union listings of provincial publications and scant alleviation of the problem through interlibrary loan co-operation. Microfilming projects are almost non-existent and even the circulation of duplicate and want lists has seldom been followed as an acquisition technique.

If there is any validity to the projections of teaching and research interest in the field presented in chapter 1, most of Canada's university libraries will be unable to meet the demands that will be placed upon them.

8
Organization of collections

The problem of how best to organize government documents has long challenged the librarian. Variation in usage, high costs of servicing, and physical difficulties of handling government publications all present major problems in collection organization and have led to a heated debate over whether or not such materials should be separated from general library collections. Libraries that have elected to separate their collections find that many other issues still remain to be settled. In particular, provincial publications present major cataloguing and classification problems.

What follows is an account of the techniques adopted by some libraries to deal with these problems. In general, the chapter merely reports, but on three issues it takes sides: from the user's point of view, the advantages of maintaining a separate documents collection outweigh the disadvantages; from the same point of view, the Guelph automated approach to cataloguing and classification is probably preferable to others, but it is only preferable if modified in one significant respect.

SEPARATE VS INTEGRATED COLLECTIONS

The basic question of whether or not government publications should be separated from the main library collection has recently been studied in depth by the University of Waterloo Library, and the resulting report,[1] while favouring separate collections, presented a balanced assessment of the advantages and disadvantages of integrated, separated, and mixed collections. In summary, integrated collections were felt to bring together on the shelves material on the same subject, regardless of origin; one catalogue can provide access to all publications in the library; a general reference staff can locate government material more quickly in an integrated collection; small libraries find integrated systems less expensive and cumbersome than separate collections. In addition, evidence suggests that libraries using integrated collections are happy with their arrangements and believe that the approach induces greater use of documents.

Countering these advantages are a host of problems peculiar to government publications, not the least of which are the problems of handling: "Documents are generally a type of material that is not easy to handle under the library's regular processing routines. Author entries are generally more complex, and many publications are non-book material such as serials and pamphlets. The maintenance of looseleaf material, and flimsy pamphlets requires special handling and attention. They also present the very real problem of volume."[2] Most libraries find it is impossible to provide full cataloguing for all the documents they receive: the expense is great, the complexity of cataloguing them forces many cataloguers to place them low on their list of priorities, and the size of the catalogue grows to unwieldy proportions. In addition, integration frequently renders government publications hard to find since it scatters interrelated material. Finally, "in the absence of a separate Documents Department, little attention is paid to a comprehensive and systematic acquisition of government documents."[3]

In contrast, the separate collection offers a higher quality of bibliographic service, is often easier to use, familiarizes users with government indexes, while simultaneously forcing novice users to consult skilled professionals whose expertise in this relatively narrow field is often very great and permits a high degree of efficiency. This promotes greater awareness of documents amongst users and, it is believed, their greater use. The library attains better control over pamphlet and ephemeral material, can save on processing costs through simplified cataloguing, and finds it easier to provide adequate facilities for handling flimsy and oversize material.

There are disadvantages, however. There is an artificial division of materials when collections are organized by issuing agency, and generally material on any one subject tends to be fragmented. A central catalogue can no longer provide access to the library's entire collection, and users have to learn how to use a variety of government indexes, a chore that discourages many. Some fear that the documents collection is often overlooked by users, and reference librarians find it difficult to keep abreast of official publications containing useful information for general inquirers. This means that the documents department must duplicate some reference services, probably at the expense of savings accrued through simplified cataloguing. Finally, it is often difficult for libraries to find sufficient space to house the entire documents collection in a convenient location.

The findings of the provincial government publishing survey corroborate those of the Waterloo study. Separate collections were generally favoured by Canadian libraries for the reasons outlined above. The Waterloo study found that "fourteen out of twenty-six reporting libraries had separate collections, with four others who would opt for separation, given choice and opportunity."[4] The provincial publishing survey discussed in interviews thirty-four libraries; eight reported integrated collections and twenty-six, separated collections. The eight include a public library, four university libraries, one government department library, one archives, and the Parliamentary Library. It is obvious that complete agreement on the way documents should be organized for most efficient use is lacking, even in one type of library.

Many of the librarians working with the collections had not been responsible for the original decisions to separate or integrate, but none expressed discontent with that decision. Those working with integrated collections were satisfied that the subject approach and attendant browsing possibilities were important to their users, and those working with separated collections were just as sure that the approach through issuing agency is superior. User needs and preferences were frequently (but not always) cited as the reason for maintaining a separate collection. When mentioned, the user was described as finding approach through issuing agency most useful and enjoying the advantages of a staff that could specialize in government documents.

The possibility of lessening costs through separating the government documents collection from the main collection has been the most important factor influencing the decision to separate. In addition, most libraries that collect provincial government documents also receive United States and Canadian federal documents. Both of the latter types come equipped with pre-assigned classification symbols and printed catalogues, which provide further approaches. If they form a separate collection, advantage can be taken of these services and the documents can be shelved immediately. Most provincial government documents have not been thus previously prepared,* but where collections are separate, they have been located with the other government documents because of the many similarities that do exist.

A few librarians reported interesting compromises between separation and integration. In at least two of the libraries discussed scientific documents are sent to science libraries because there is heavy demand for them there, but a union list of government documents is kept in the government documents section. The University of British Columbia Library has a collection that is mainly integrated but provides some special treatment. Current serials not yet ready to be bound and items difficult to catalogue are kept in the government documents division, as is a union list of all government documents that have come into the library since 1965.

*There are some exceptions to this generalization. Most provincial departments of agriculture use the Agdex classification system in their check-lists. This system is in common use in the United States. It is based on subject analysis and applies only to items of an agricultural nature. The Quebec Queen's Printer in his check-lists provides notation symbols for issuing departments.

CATALOGUING AND CLASSIFICATION SYSTEMS

Most of the libraries surveyed handle provincial documents in separate collections, then proceed to invest in them the minimum of services. A typical collection has no references to it in the main card catalogue; there is only a shelf list or kardex to assist the user before he applies to the librarian in charge for help. Documents are filed alphabetically by issuing agency, but details such as what system is followed when government structure changes are not outlined for the user. He has few reference tools to turn to. Bibliographies such as Hazel MacTaggart's[5] give short histories of departments, but ready reference histories of government structures are in most cases non-existent. An attempt to remedy this situation was begun as a supplement to *Canadiana* but never completed.

Those who work in separate collections described the user as a faculty member or a graduate student. This description is further supported by many faculty members, who commented that limited availability of provincial government documents had not restricted the scope of undergraduate courses because students in these were directed to secondary sources, a statement that contrasts strangely with the widely recognized dearth of secondary sources in the field. One librarian defined the graduate student further as one who had been sent by a faculty member who had studied the collection and told the student what to look for. This well-informed user was often the reason cited for providing the minimum number of tools for access; however, one is forced to wonder who adapted first - the library to the users' needs or the users to the library conditions. Librarians working in integrated collections did not volunteer any information about the types of people using their documents.

There are, however, some exceptions to the typical collection described above. A few libraries do provide extra cataloguing and classification services. Some have added title catalogues.* Others reported full conventional cataloguing. Of these, one special library reported skeletal title and subject cards (with extensive subject work) and found this method successful. A university library reported that full cataloguing created too great a work load for the government documents division to handle and was going to be dropped for the simplified approach adopted by the University of Guelph Documentation Centre for its automated catalogues. Publisher, place of publication, and collation are omitted and KWIC† indexing is substituted for the use of L.C. subject headings. Officials at the University of Guelph claim that because their system also does not require decisions as to main entry or cataloguing format,‡ "for prototype materials ... an intelligent high school graduate with a few days training can code

---

*One librarian mentioned using *Canadiana* as a reference tool, since it has a title approach.
†Key word in context.
‡All entries are main entries. Required information is transcribed onto a form sheet.

50 documents a day as compared with 15 or 20 a day by the crack professional librarian following the more rigid cataloging practices."[6]

Subject listing by KWIC was adopted for the following reasons: "We feel that in the first place the LC Subject Headings are too general to be of any real help. Secondly, if we are to adopt or develop any special thesaurus, it would be too costly and too time consuming to do a faithful job of subject analysing and subject indexing. Each subject field requires its own experts. The average librarians are simply not equipped to cope with it."[7] At Guelph, selection of key words is limited to those found in the title.

Some libraries have devised classification schemes. The library used by personnel in the Office of the Economic Advisor in New Brunswick has been arranged according to the Dominion Bureau of Statistics classification, which is based on subject. However, since one of the reasons for keeping the collection separate was to eliminate the expensive process of detailed classification by subject, which the Dominion Bureau of Statistics, L.C., and Dewey systems require, most of the systems devised have been based on issuing agency.

Mrs Judith Colson at the Harriet Irving Library, University of New Brunswick, is adapting Ellen Jackson's *Notation for a Public Documents Classification*[8] to fit Canadian provincial documents.

A detailed alpha-numeric scheme has been drawn up for Quebec documents by M. André Beaulieu of Laval University Library;[9] the letters stand for names of departments and the numbers for types of publications issued by a department. The letter symbols have been adopted by the Queen's Printer (Quebec) and were used by Mrs Rombough in her *Classification Outline for Canadian Provincial Documents*[10] mentioned below. M. Beaulieu developed his scheme after studying the classification systems of the United States Government's Official Documents Division and Ellen Jackson's studies: *A Manual for the Administration of the Federal Documents*[11] and *Notation for a Public Documents Classification*. In his words, "Dans une certaine mésure l'élaboration de cette classification se réclame des études mentionnées."

Mr Lan Sun of Guelph University Documentation Center describes the classification system developed and applied there:

The following diagram shows the structure of the document number, or the classification scheme.

Country	Part	Province or State	Major Organization	Subdivision	Year of Public.	Title		Emergency Digit
A	A	N	A A	A A	N N	N N	A N N	N
1	2	3	4 5	6 7	8 9	10 11	12 13 14	15

(The numerals indicate the number of digits. The letter A, or N, on top of the numerals indicates the digit is either alphabetic or numeric.)

For example, if the Idaho Agricultural Experiment Station has been established in our file as the corporate author and assigned US2IDU12 (read US†2-ID-U-12, where US is the country code for the United States, 2 indicates part 2, ie. States, ID is the code for the State of Idaho, U is the organization code and here stands for the University of Idaho, 12 represents Department-12 and here stands for the Agricultural Experiment Station) as its organization code (our classification number), then all the publications issued by this station will have this same classification number ... The differentiating elements in the document number are now reduced to the date of publication (year) and the title (simplified Cutter number).[12]

Another arrangement within the Guelph program has been developed by Mrs Beatrice Rombough at the Douglas Library, Queen's University. It was decided after study of the Guelph scheme that a different arrangement would be more useful at the Douglas Library; for instance, shelving royal commissions together was preferred to having them classified by subject. Mrs Rombough describes her *Classification Outline for Canadian Provincial Documents* as "in general an alphabetical arrangement within each province, modelled on the [federal Queen's Printer's] *Outline of Classification for Canadian Government Publications.*"

According to a scheme devised by D. Tudor, librarian with the Ontario Department of Revenue, a collection of government documents can be categorized into legislative and non-legislative materials. Non-legislative materials are treated in the same fashion as books and periodicals, while legislative materials are divided into eight types:

1 Statutes, bills, statutory regulations, etc.
2 Debates, journals, etc., of the Lower House
3 Debates, journals, etc., of the Upper House
4 Committee reports
5 Royal Commissions (shelved by date of order in council, or some other legislative authority)
6 Annual reports of departments
7 Budget statement, estimates, public accounts
8 Gazette

Each number is appended to an abbreviation of the jurisdiction (e.g., Ontario 1, Ontario statutes; Ontario 8, Ontario *Gazette*) and further subdivisions are indicated by Cuttering the necessary number of times. Mr Tudor feels that the advantages of this scheme are that the items he considers the most important sections of government publishing (legislative materials) can be kept together on a small basis and can be shelved easily because most are continuations.[13]

In addition to all the problems connected with servicing a provincial document collection, there remains the fact that even if that collection is rendered all the card catalogues usually provided a book collection, it is still relatively inaccessible to the user because of the complexity of the material, the lack of indexes, and the general lack of readily available information on the history or workings of provincial governments. Sophisticated reference tools are badly needed.

For the work that must be done in separate libraries servicing individual collections, automation provides interesting new possibilities.

AUTOMATION

Guelph University Library has pioneered in the application of computer technology to the "organization, control, and retrieval" of a document collection. In 1966 the University established a Documentation Centre with the aim of devising "a simple, comparatively inexpensive method ... to organize and control government publications and technical reports, making access to them available through the shelves, card catalog or book lists, and providing some method of informing research workers in advance of specified need of publications in their field of interest."[14]

The output of the system is one shelf list and the following public service catalogues: (1) corporate author and title catalogue, (2) personal author index, (3) title listing, (4) series listing, (5) serials listing, and (6) subject list by KWIC.*[15] To achieve this output, these bibliographic elements of a publication are considered essential: (1) corporate author, (2) second corporate author, (3) indistinctive title, (4) first distinctive title, (5) second distinctive title, (6) personal author(s) (A maximum of 3 personal authors are allowed for each document), (7) numbering statement, if a serial, (8) series, (9) edition or revision statement, (10) date of publication, (11) necessary notes.[16] The collection is organized according to the scheme described above and is housed "under fairly strict control, with browsing possible for such documents as debates, statutes, etc."[17]

Mr Sun points out that the system could be used by governments to produce listings of their publications. For example:

We assigned the organization code of CA2ONAF ... to the Ontario Department of Agriculture and Food. If we ask the computer to extract all the documents bearing that code (columns 12 to 18 in the header card) and run through the catalogue programs, we would have a complete set of 6 catalogues for all the publications in our collection issued by that organization ... If all government agencies would send us their publications as soon as they publish them, we would provide them our free listing service for their own publications. This scheme can of course be expanded to any other organization, and can be

---

*Unfortunately the KWIC subject list has had to await development of a program suitable for the IBM 360 computer used by the Centre.

developed into a provincial or national center for the most prompt listing services of all current government publications, which or lack of which has been a major concern of the users as well as the library personnel.[18]

Even without the KWIC index the Guelph system compares favourably with traditional systems. The user finds that a book catalogue is less cumbersome, and therefore quicker, than the traditional card catalogue[19] and exchange of collection information between libraries is facilitated.[20] Introduction of the KWIC index should provide a much more flexible subject approach than has been possible through traditional methods. When we consider that some libraries applying Library of Congress subject headings to government documents have been forced by the costs involved to modify the subject headings drastically, we cannot help but conclude that an approach using co-ordinate indexing is peculiarly applicable in the government documents library.

However, there are limitations to the Guelph system as currently applied. From the user's point of view, the most serious difficulty stems from the fact that, even with co-ordinate indexing, access to much of the collection will be less than might be expected of the system. This is not to deny that the system is an improvement on earlier approaches: it simply suggests that if a new technology is to be employed, then it should be fully exploited. The Guelph approach does not make sufficiently extensive use of co-ordinate indexing. By incorporating only permuted title indexing in the system, it closes off access to the entire range of subordinate documents that are included in most government serials. The problem is similar to that of applying KWIC indexing to periodical articles, although it is rendered less complicated by the fact that most government agencies have relatively few words in their names. By indexing the table of contents of annual reports, for example, the system could vastly improve accessibility to the collection.

The case for such a modification of the system rests on the fact that many users find existing collections of government documents virtually unmanageable as sources of comparative data. Governments are so complex and agencies are so large and multifaceted, that the name of an agency gives very limited information concerning its function. Mr Lan Sun maintains that "subject classification is implied in our method of organization, because each government organization will be expected to publish material more or less in the subject field defined by its official functions."[21] But the user cannot establish "official functions" from the catalogue; he must consult the reference department. There he finds that adequate guides to functions do not always exist and that it is often virtually impossible to track down in a short time a responsibility centre in a jurisdiction that is unfamiliar to him. He finds himself browsing at random through the publications of unfamiliar jurisdictions, consulting statutes, or giving up in despair. KWIC indexing of tables of contents would cost the library more, perhaps, but would save the scholar vast quantities of time and effort. It might make possible extensive developments in comparative studies, forestalled at present by the Herculean task of locating information resources.

NOTES

1 / Rienzi W.G. Cruzz, *Organization and Management of Government Documents: An Investigation with Special Reference to the University of Waterloo Libraries* (Waterloo, Ontario: Reference Department, Dana Porter Arts Library, University of Waterloo, 9 Oct. 1969).
2 / *Ibid.*, 14.
3 / *Ibid.*, 16,
4 / *Ibid.*, 24.
5 / Hazel MacTaggart, *Publications of the Government of Ontario, 1901-1955* (Toronto: University of Toronto Press for the Queen's Printer, 1964).
6 / Lan Sun, *The Documentation Centre of the University of Guelph Library: a Report Prepared for the Panel Discussion of the Ontario Library Association, Ontario Resources and Technical Services Group, Fall Workshop, Held at the Memorial Hall, University of Guelph, October 28, 1967* (mimeo.), 41.
7 / *Ibid.*, 5.
8 / Stillwater, 1946.
9 / André Beaulieu, *Projet de classification des publications gouvernementales du Québec* (mimeo.).
10 / Mimeo.
11 / Chicago, 1955.
12 / Sun, "The Documentation Centre," 3.
13 / Letter to A.P. Pross, 7 Aug. 1969.
14 / Beckman, Margaret, "A Documentation Centre at the University of Guelph Library," *Ontario Library Review* (Dec. 1966), 226-9.
15 / Sun, "The Documentation Centre," 4.
16 / *Ibid.*, 3.
17 / Beckman, "A Documentation Centre," 227.
18 / Sun, "The Documentation Centre," 6.
19 / F.W. Matthews and D.L. Oulton, "A Simplified Computer Produced Book Catalogue." (In *Proceedings - American Documentation Institute*, IV 1967. 191-6.) Page 191 refers to this aspect of computer catalogues and cites other authorities.
20 / Sun, "The Documentation Centre," 5.
21 / *Ibid.*, 2.

9
The underdeveloped role of provincial legislative libraries

The legislative libraries are pivotal elements in the business of studying the politics, economics, and sociology of Canada's provinces. Their collections are the most extensive available. Too frequently - in view of the fire hazard - they are unique. Their staff are usually few in number, yet exceptionally well informed and capable of quickly leading the academic or governmental researcher to the most fruitful sources. The library community depends on them to an inordinate extent. Without their dedication to document discovery few provincial publications would be listed in *Canadiana,* and without their advice and intercession the publications themselves would seldom be placed on the shelves of university and public libraries. In addition, far too many university libraries count on neighbouring legislative collections to supply the research needs of faculty and students. Finally, the extent of their commitment to parliamentary government is evidenced by each late-night sitting of the legislature and the care with which meagre resources are husbanded so that members may be properly served.

Yet they are capable of far more. Their collections could be better used; their reference staff could perform infinitely more important functions in assisting legislators, administrators, academics, and the general public, and the services they perform for the library community could be rendered much more complete if provincial budgets gave them sufficient funds for the logical and necessary extension of current activities.

Before elaborating this proposition at length, it is worthwhile describing the general features of the provincial legislative library systems.

No province is without its legislative library, although their size and physical characteristics vary, from that of Newfoundland, which is located in a single moderate-sized room and is not extensive, to that of British Columbia, which acts as the core of the provincial library system and is housed in quarters whose grandeur almost compensates for their inconvenience. All the libraries possess a common feature: they are under-utilized.

It was not possible to gather reliable data to support or disprove this view, and it consequently remains a highly subjective one. Nevertheless, interviews with civil servants and librarians lend it some support. Not all librarians are as worried as one who spent some time discussing the gradual erosion of the responsibilities of the library and the increasing difficulty in obtaining appropriations to cover the costs of hiring competent staff. Not all provincial civil servants view the provincial legislative library as a tourist attraction and resort to the nearest university library as the source of their research data. But the interviews conducted in the course of carrying out the survey suggest that a significant number of librarians and civil servants do feel this way.

How has this come about? Part of the answer lies in the nineteenth century, which saw the building of these libraries and, to a degree, the legislative systems which utilized them. It is interesting, though possibly not significant, that in the nine legislative buildings built in the public architecture traditions of the eighteenth and nineteenth centuries, the library occupies a place of importance and is physically impressive. In Newfoundland, whose Confederation Building is rendered in a functional style that is reminiscent of socialist realism, the library is tucked away in a room that could, with greater convenience, have housed a typing pool. Does the twentieth-century legislator attach any less significance to researching his subject than his predecessors? Probably not, but his style of oratory has changed. He no longer relies heavily on a classical-humanist library to feed his speeches. He looks instead to the type of document that we have suggested does not find its way into the library: the departmental or pressure-group study. He frequently feels he can more adequately fill this need by maintaining personal contacts with government officials, newspapermen, pressure-group representatives, and party members than by exploiting the resources of the library. In addition, his attempts to use the library may prove abortive. Library reference work requires a skill possessed by few members of the general public, and most of the provincial legislative libraries are too inadequately staffed to provide the type of reference service that encourages repeated use. A further factor limiting library use by members is the extreme complexity of much legislation. Many writers have commented on the difficulties this poses for the average legislator, but few provinces provide the type of research assistance needed to meet the problem.

Thus, many legislators remain unaware of the potential usefulness of libraries created, in some instances, solely for their benefit. It is hardly surprising, then, that legislative librarians have long had cause to complain of their meagre appropriations. What is surprising is that most legislative libraries fare as well as they do.

One would expect the provincial civil service, increasingly staffed with professionals, to fill the vacuum left by the legislators. On the whole, this has not happened for a variety of reasons. The first stems from the fact that many agencies, having outgrown the facilities originally provided and having relocated some distance from the legislature, either have made less use of the library's resources or have built their own small collections. In most cases such libraries are inadequately staffed and have no contact with the legislative library. The legislative library has in turn felt itself challenged by the departmental libraries but has had neither the resources to provide either the sort of reference or book delivery service that would obviate the need they fill, nor the means to take departmental libraries under its wing.

A second reason for the poor use made of the library by civil servants lies in the fact that the library has been built as an imposing edifice, not as a place for reading and research. The properly trained researcher used to the facilities of the better university libraries will soon be discouraged by those of most Canadian legislative libraries. Although these comments do not apply in their entirety to all of the provincial legislative libraries, there are in most no separate carrel areas, no facilities for typing notes, no easy chairs for relaxed reading. Instead, the researcher must share a long, not always well-lit, table with one or two other users; he may not smoke, let alone type; and he must be prepared for periodic interruptions by gaggles of tourists who, tired of admiring architecture, examine him with apathetic interest. Even the photo-copying equipment now available in nearly all university, public, and archival libraries is lacking here.

A third cause of civil service neglect of the legislative library resources has to be attributed to the poor research education the universities accord the majority of their graduates. There seems to be a conviction amongst university educators that only students intending to enter professional academic work need receive intensive training in research techniques. Such training usually begins at the post-graduate level, one not always reached by those entering the civil service. Undergraduates are too frequently equipped with extensive bibliographies by their professors, armed with which they search card catalogues for call numbers to a few titles, then browse the selected classification range for those and related titles. The reference librarian is seldom called upon to help, and the student is never introduced to the techniques of using a reference collection. When he graduates, the student is usually aware of the library, but untrained in its proper use. As a civil servant he tends to find himself lost in the legislative library, particularly if he is not used to the classification system. The library's lack of staff makes it difficult to obtain the reference assistance he needs, and, inevitably, library research becomes an activity he avoids. As a substitute, he builds a small, poorly selected collection within his department. Here he feels at home; he can continue to use the sloppy research techniques he has developed in university and he soon forgets that the knowledge he gains from the small and inadequate collection ready to hand is not all that is needed to advise his government.

There are other reasons for lack of bureaucratic use of legislative library resources: many civil servants prefer using the nearest university library because it is more familiar to them, it is sometimes a better collection, it enables the civil servant to maintain contact with the university community, and sometimes it is simply a more prestigious library to use. In a few interviews, civil servants reported feeling that the legislative library was not for their use, but for the use of the legislature alone. Finally, laziness and ignorance also play their part. In very few instances is civil service neglect of the legislative library attributable to the fact that the collection is inadequate. In most cases the legislative library contains the best collection of material available dealing with the province concerned. It usually lacks the breadth found in most university collections, but in depth it is often so much better that it is regularly used by academics. Thus we find that academics, who know how to use libraries, prefer the legislative library to their own, whilst civil servants, poorly trained in library techniques, use the more readily accessible university collection.

To anyone concerned about the quality of advice tendered government policy makers, the foregoing catalogue is profoundly depressing. In each province one of the best stocked "data banks" available is being under-utilized because library staff cannot service the potential user community, because the physical facilities available to the would-be user are inadequate or inappropriate, because too few users possess the skills they need to retrieve the information the collection contains, and because inadequate departmental libraries are being used as substitutes for the much richer collection available in the legislative library.

It is possible that a partial solution to these problems might also overcome the problem of discovering what the provincial governments are publishing. Such a solution would encompass: (a) developing a reference research group within the legislative library which could contribute personnel to serve as members of agency research teams, and (b) integration of departmental libraries in a governmental library system. If successfully applied these measures could achieve: (a) optimum utilization of legislative library resources, (b) a more extensive flow of information to administrative researchers, (c) a versatile and competent reference staff skilled in providing governments with adequate information in the shortest possible time, and (d) a continuous flow of information concerning government publications to the Canadian library community and thence to the academic and general public.

It is difficult to estimate the size of staff needed to carry out the functions that will be outlined. However, we might suppose that a group of half a dozen professional librarians divide the reference work of the various government agencies among them. One might be responsible for the related activities of finance and economic development, another for the natural resource departments, another for attorney-general and provincial secretary, and so on. It would be the responsibility of the librarian to acquaint himself with the work and history of each department before attempting to offer his services to it. Having learned enough to convince the department that he is not an utter incompetent, he would initiate contact at several levels, including: (1) letters to the minister, deputy minister, and key officials advising that a reference service geared to the needs of the department has been instituted, (2) a personal visit to follow up the letter and elaborate details, (3) circulation of bibliographic documents such as "recent acquisitions" and bibliographies of materials relating to specific research activities of departmental branches and sections, (4) compilation of research profiles of principal researchers within the department (this activity would involve personal interviews that would provide the opportunity to gather necessary information and to educate the researcher to make greater use of the new reference service), and (5) circulation to individuals within the department of materials geared to their research interests. Thus each researcher would periodically receive bibliographies of materials related to his interests and from time to time might receive photo-copies of recent journal articles of interest to him as well as notification of the arrival in the library of new publications.

The limited experience of such a scheme that was reported[1] suggests that the department and the library will gradually build up an effective working relationship in which the librarian figures as a key member of the research or advisory group. This has occurred in Ontario where Mr S. Bene of the Department of Trade and Development and Mr D. Tudor of the Department of Treasury and Economics and Department of Revenue provide several of the services described above and have won the unstinted praise of the research staff.

Effective implementation of such a scheme would do much to overcome present problems in identifying provincial publications. Legislative libraries, the principal suppliers of information concerning provincial documents, would be able to perform this function with greater exactitude and promptness by virtue of the fact that library staff would be aware of research leading to publication and thus better able to ensure deposition of the finished product. Arrangements similar to those currently in effect at the British Columbia Legislative Library and the Newfoundland Public Archives[2] could ensure that confidential documents, or documents yet to be made public, would be deposited but would be treated separately from public documents. Such an arrangement might promote the development of a consistent policy for release of documents, since one agency, the legislative library, would develop primary responsibility for meeting public requests for such documents and would thus be in a position to propose, and press for, policy development.

The proliferation of departmental book collections in various provincial administrations has caused concern to treasury officials and to professional librarians at the legislative library level. To treasury officials, the problem presented by such growth is one of cost. They fear the duplication of the legislative library's collection and they realize that the costs of servicing the departmental collections, some of which are extensive, may be unnecessary. Essentially, the cost problems involved are the same as those applying in the case of departments wishing to publish their own documents. Essentially, too, the reasons for wishing to do so and for permitting the growth of such library services are the same: the central facility is felt to be inadequate.

Professional librarians point out that in addition to cost factors, the departmental operation frequently provides low-quality service. Staff is not trained in book selection, cataloguing, or reference work. As a result, departmental library collections are frequently inferior, reflecting the whims of researchers in the department and not the orderly and meaningful development of a collection that can be achieved by a good subject specialist. Catalogue access to such collections is usually poor; sometimes it is almost non-existent and the collection is accessible only to those who know it well. The reference service provided seldom amounts to more than the ability to point out the location of a book on the shelves, a service usually provided by a good public catalogue.*

Despite the validity of the professional librarian's complaint, he is far from winning his case. This is chiefly because usually the only alternative he offers is the legislative library itself, and the departments have already fled that facility. In this respect the position of the librarian is little different from that of the Queen's Printer or any other central service judged inadequate.

Our proposals for improved reference service should meet the problem in part. However, as long as legislative libraries are housed in their present quarters and as long as the various departments are not within easy walking distance, pressure for the creation of departmental collections will grow.

There are several steps that can be taken to meet the problem. Depending on the needs of the various departments, they would include:

(a) provision of fast pick-up and delivery service from the central library to individual users,
(b) creation of a central union list for all books owned by the government,
(c) co-ordination of departmental services with those of the central library so that the central library would have responsibility for:
   (i) book ordering,
   (ii) cataloguing,
   (iii) collection review,
   (iv) interlibrary loan,
   (v) reference,

whilst the departmental operation, under the supervision of a library technician would be responsible for:
   (i) public catalogue maintenance,
   (ii) general duties within the library.

*Mr Tudor points out that "in Ontario there is not one 'departmental' library that is not under the guidance of a professional librarian. Any libraries that are looked after by clerks are for branches ... The ... Treasury Board is doing a comprehensive survey of Civil Service Libraries and we hope to eliminate duplication of subject fields and ensure more co-operation." Letter to P. Pross, 7 August 1969.

There would be some shared responsibilities, notably:
  (i) an experienced library technician would be able to handle routine reference questions
  (ii) the library technician would frequently be in a position to collect acquisition requests from research staffs.

Where the department has an extensive operation, it would be desirable to install a full-time professional librarian who would, however, maintain a close liaison with the central library. More generally, however, an effective agent for co-ordinating the activities of the central and departmental library would be the reference librarian assigned to assist departmental researchers. Fully aware of the agency's research activity, frequently in contact with individual members of the department and familiar with the literature required, he would be uniquely equipped to appreciate the department's needs and to provide meaningful direction to the clerical staff providing most of the necessary technical services. At the same time, through maintaining a base in the central library, he would bring to his relations with the department an extensive knowledge of the central collection and an ability to utilize services that might not otherwise be brought to departmental attention. Finally, through his knowledge of the literature and the needs of the departmental research group, the librarian would be in a position to periodically weed the departmental collection, sending little-used volumes to the central collection and thus helping to ensure maximum utilization of individual volumes, whilst equipping the departmental library with needed current and standard literature and at the same time keeping the departmental collection within manageable proportions.

It is not immediately apparent that this discussion of the plight of most of Canada's provincial legislative libraries, together with recommendations, promotes improved acquisition of provincial government publications by other libraries. Nevertheless, given the possibility that production and distribution of publications may be decentralized for years to come, the legislative libraries then, as now, will act as the most competent authorities to advise the library community in general of the existence of specific publications. This is a crucially important function in a field of public information where bibliographical guide posts are scanty. It follows, then, that any procedure that enables the legislative library to ascertain the existence of publications is worth considering for implementation. It is suggested that the procedures put forward here would not only lead to an improvement in the quality of advice tendered provincial governments, it would ensure continuous contact between the librarian and those responsible for preparing documents for publication. Such contacts represent the surest possible access to information concerning proposed government publications and to acquisition of the documents themselves.

It is unfortunate that much of this outline of the situation currently existing within provincial legislative library systems may give the impression that the deficiencies described are attributable to poor administration on the part of the legislative librarians. Nothing could be farther from the truth. Against steadily mounting odds, Canada's legislative librarians have succeeded in serving not only their legislatures and governments, but also the broader Canadian community of government, university, and public libraries. Overwhelmed as they have been, it is hardly surprising that they have been unable to exert the consistent pressure that will be needed if major improvements are to be sanctioned by the governments concerned.

Furthermore, they seem to have been hampered by a gentlemanly reluctance to exploit their close relationships with many legislators in order to engage in the competitive self-seeking that is the rule amongst most agencies. L. Quincy Mumford, the Librarian of Congress, has described their predicament best:

A public administrator is always confronted with the problem of balancing the various elements of his own internal program, and also the representation of his needs against other claims on the general treasury. The Library of Congress is inherently in an awkward position in advancing its own claims for congressional support. Scholarly objectivity commingles poorly with the vigorous pursuit of claims for self-preferment. We can scarcely advise the Congress as to the importance of our institution to the Congress. It would be effrontery to dwell on the usefulness of an institution to those who are among its principal users.[3]

Finally, their role in the parliamentary system militates against them. Members are glad enough of their assistance when in opposition, reluctant to improve the service when in government. Consequently, while most legislative libraries have many friends at court, their champions are few and usually impotent. A key to improvement lies in developing the services available to the bureaucracy, as we have suggested. In addition, it is the responsibility of their friends in the academic and library communities to provide the pressure needed to win for the provincial legislative libraries the governmental support required to maintain and improve services that are crucial to the effective governing of this country.

NOTES

1 / Interviews with Mr S. Bene, Director, Library and Records Management Branch, Ontario Department of Trade and Development; Mr D. Tudor, Librarian, Ontario Department of Revenue, and Mr S. Smith, Ontario Department of Treasury and Economics.
2 / Documents are deposited but not released until tabled or otherwise made public.
3 / In John Lear,"Technology's Assessors," *Saturday Review*, 25 April 1970, 52.

10
Recommendations

No one formula can overcome the problems that have been described in the preceding chapters. It will not be possible to standardize production and distribution of provincial government publications throughout the country. The great differences in resources and needs of the various provinces preclude neat solutions.

The following recommendations are proposed in the awareness of these restrictions. In as many cases as possible alternative proposals are put forward, in the hope that where a province's resources cannot encompass one solution, they will another. In addition, proposals are not confined to the governmental level; there is much that can be done by the many interested libraries.

In our introductory chapter we suggested that five fundamental problems permeate the provincial government publications "situation." These five problems are:
1 The need for a clear definition of a provincial government publication;
2 The haphazard nature of government structures for processing and distributing publications;
3 The absence of adequate procedures for the "discovery" of publications;
4 The lack of an effective depository system;
5 The deficient library procedures for handling documents, including inadequate arrangements for reporting and locating documents and failure to devise systems for the retrieval of the information they contain.

In an attempt to encase a wide variety of recommendations in a semblance of order, they are presented as solutions to each of the five problems identified. We move first to deal with the problem of definition, then to the problem of decentralization, and so on, concluding with a group of lesser proposals and some suggestions for appropriate action on the part of the Canadian Political Science Association and other interested groups. A summary orders the recommendations on a priority basis and suggests where initiatives might start.

1. THE NEED FOR A CLEAR DEFINITION OF A PROVINCIAL GOVERNMENT PUBLICATION

In chapter 2 we pointed out that a reasonable definition could be arrived at through public debate, and suggested that a government publication might be described as: *any document prepared by or for any agency of government and reproduced and circulated to groups and individuals other than those advising or negotiating with the government concerning the subject matter of the document.*

We are convinced, however, that until a specific administrator has been given the duty and incentive to implement the definition by applying classification rules in an equitable fashion, it is unlikely that general recognition of any definition will improve conditions. It is important to evolve definitions, but we must also take into account the realities of administrative life, and organizational behaviour is such that unless it is in the self-interest of one particular official to apply the definition in the desired manner, no paper formula will have any effect.

We therefore recommend *that each jurisdiction appoint a responsible official - a Supervisor of Documents - to examine all government documents reproduced in significant quantity and to determine, in conjunction with publishing departments, which documents should circulate only within the government, which should be sent to depository research libraries, which to general depository libraries, and which should receive broad public distribution.*

The Supervisor of Documents should be attached to an agency in which public as well as bureaucratic influences can be felt. The legislative library or the office of the official publisher might provide such an administrative home. The location will largely depend on the capacity of the governmental structure to provide him with copies of all the documents reproduced in significant quantity. Where appreciable centralization of photo-copying exists, he could fairly easily be supplied with copies of all documents processed by the system. Elsewhere he might require extensive assistance in document discovery and his office might consequently be attached to the legislative library.

It is important that he not be treated as a subordinate of the director of the agency providing the administrative home and document review facilities. The Supervisor of Documents would have to have sufficient independence to exercise impartial judgment in classification of documents. Consequently, his decisions must be his alone or else those of an over-riding authority, such as that of the minister of the department issuing any given publication. He must not be vulnerable to subtle pressures from an immediate superior who is not obviously responsible for classification decisions.

Nevertheless, it would be unrealistic to expect agencies to accept the judgment of such an official as binding. Circumventing devices can soon render an administrator with too much power as impotent as the man who has none at all, and a Supervisor of Documents imbued with arbitrary authority to determine the degree of publicity given any departmental document would be bound to earn immediate agency opposition. A compromise might establish a procedure that would allow the issuing agency initial responsibility for determining classification. This classification would be reviewed by the Supervisor of Documents, who would negotiate revisions with the agency concerned, but would be bound to submit to the decision of the minister in charge of the department should an impasse develop.

In summary, the Supervisor of Documents would be empowered to review all government documents reproduced in significant quantity and to indicate to distributing agencies the breadth of circulation to be accorded to each item. While he himself would have considerable freedom from bureaucratic pressures, his decisions would be subject to negotiation with issuing agencies and, if necessary, review at the ministerial level.

2. THE HAPHAZARD NATURE OF GOVERNMENT STRUCTURES FOR PROCESSING AND DISTRIBUTING PUBLICATIONS

Many familiar with the difficulties of the present system have urged strongly that all provincial governments centralize their production and distribution arrangements. There are two reasons why this is not as attractive a solution as appears at first sight. First, experience has shown that centralization does not necessarily achieve its purpose. An inefficient central operation can introduce greater problems than those it was created to overcome and forces those dependent upon it to seek alternatives to the central services. The end result may be greater decentralization, confusion, and expense than had existed before the remedy was applied. Second, centralization will not, in the short run at least, achieve appreciable savings. These and other considerations are investigated in chapters 3 and 4.

Despite the recognized disadvantages of centralization, there are occasions when the benefits are great enough to outweigh them. The merits of centralizing printing facilities have been recognized in several jurisdictions for some time; similar measures for the production of processed documents are long overdue. Centralization in this field would not prohibit installation of low-capacity copying equipment wherever needed, but it would prevent bulk copying at all but one level. The disadvantages of such an arrangement include the possibility that monopoly will create an inefficient and unco-operative service, which might discourage in turn the processing and printing of materials that should receive limited but public circulation and eventually lead agencies to return to decentralized production practices. The system holds the advantage of eliminating the current wasteful practice of over-producing publication print runs on office copiers and of reducing under-utilization of equipment. In other words, copying will be carried out on machinery capable of providing the required number of copies at the most economical price. For the user, centralization holds out the possibility that an efficient structure could be created to facilitate the flow of documentation to libraries serving him.

In order to minimize the disadvantages of centralization at this level, a suitable service philosophy should be adopted. That is, it should be the objective of every service agency to ensure that every department receives a service that is at least as good as it could provide for itself and that most departments receive much better service. No agency should be coerced into using the central service; it should be convinced, and having been convinced, it should retain the option of restoring its own service should the central facility fail to live up to expectations. Furthermore, centralization of function should not mean centralization of facility. If agencies request location of facilities close to hand, then every effort should be made to meet their requests. Only if the inefficiency and arrogance of monopoly can be avoided will centralization at this level be meaningful. Bearing these pitfalls in mind, we recommend *that all provincial governments be urged to centralize all multi-copying and printing services.*

Centralization of mailing facilities is another area in which the advantages of centralization outweigh the disadvantages. Equipment is available that permits rapid updating of lists as well as extremely efficient distribution of bulk mailings. Here, again, the central service agency would have a responsibility to provide as good or better service than user agencies are capable of achieving. Given the efficiency of much modern equipment we recommend *that all provincial governments be encouraged to centralize their bulk mailing facilities.*

It is a short step from centralizing the facility to creating a single master mailing list for each province. This step is not easily achieved, however. Certain agencies believe that their mailing lists have to be carefully tended by high level personnel. For example, departments of trade and industry attempt to direct distribution so precisely that the busy executive never receives an irrelevant publication and is thus more receptive to the selected publications which are sent to him. Officials fear that inclusion of their lists in a master list would lead to abuse of this communications device and bury essential specific literature in a mass of irrelevant publications.[1] Again, such agencies wish to screen lists because they do not want to "waste" expensive publications on recipients who are not likely to invest in the province and also because they believe certain confidential publications should receive only extremely limited circulation. The strength of these objections, and those who put them forward, is reflected in the Ontario government's decision to centralize operation of mailing facilities but not control of mailing lists themselves. The problem centralization of mailing lists poses for the user has been described in chapter 4.

Despite these difficulties, we believe that efforts should be made to establish provincial master lists for distribution purposes. We feel that with adequate supervision from competent administrators, master lists can be devised to reflect the widely varying needs of user agencies and those wishing to receive publications. The structure of such a list could be similar to the sophisticated list described in chapter 3 and could be flexible enough to permit agencies to isolate certain categories of readers from receiving general mailings, while providing for distribution of the widest possible range of publications to research libraries. Such lists would have to be maintained under the supervision of a qualified administrator aware of the list's role in the process of public communications and of the needs of the user agencies. We therefore recommend *that provincial governments be urged to:* (1) *establish provincial master lists for use in the distribution of publications;* (2) *provide for adequate administration of the lists through the appointment of an appropriate official.* In addition, we recommend *that provincial governments be urged to advise recipients when mailings lists are being revised and request them to indicate whether or not they wish to remain on the lists.*[2]

Whilst centralization of production and mailing facilities is feasible in all provinces, extensive centralization of distribution appears to be possible only in Quebec, Ontario, and British Columbia. The Quebec experience has shown that demand for the publications of the provincial government is great enough to sustain a fairly extensive operation. It is clear that the Government of Ontario believes that a similar facility should exist in that province. British Columbia as the third richest and most populous province should be able to afford a similar service. We recommend *that the governments of Quebec, Ontario, and British Columbia be encouraged to establish, or extend, policies of centralized distribution.* Furthermore, we recommend *that the central distributing agency - the Official Publisher - have responsibility for:* (1) *operating a government publications bookstore,* (2) *providing bibliographic services for the province's publications,* (3) *depositing provincial publications in selected libraries in the province and elsewhere,* (4) *providing an administrative home for the Supervisor of Documents' office.*

A provincial government bookstore could be centrally located in the provincial capital and branches might be operated in other major cities (e.g., Victoria and Vancouver; Toronto and Ottawa; Quebec and Montreal). Stock for sale could include annual reports, royal commission reports, the public accounts, legislative debates, statutes, special studies, and so on. Free literature could also be made available. It is suggested that a nominal charge be applied to the bulk of provincial publications distributed by the bookstore. This would diminish the waste in distributing certain publications. For example, in several provinces officials feel that members of the public sometimes ask for the *Public Accounts* more for the sake of discovering a neighbour's salary than for studying government spending policies. The bookstore would also operate a mail-order branch.

Under the head of "bibliographic services" is included a variety of activity ranging from regular publication of brochures of publications available and weekly or monthly check-lists to compilation of retrospective bibliographies, cataloguing, and KWIC indexing of publications, and the production of catalogue cards for libraries served by the system. Some of these activities are not usually provided by government publishers, although a number are provided or envisioned in the Ontario and Quebec systems. However, despite the costs these services would incur, provincial governments would benefit considerably. Not only would accessibility of information be improved, but much costly duplication of effort found in university library processing systems would be eliminated.

The responsibility of the Official Publisher would include not only the task of ensuring that depositories would automatically receive the publication to which they were entitled, it would also include the responsibility of recommending to the provincial government the names of libraries to be accorded depository status and the conditions for holding that status. Presumably, neither the Official Publisher nor the libraries concerned would wish policy to be established without adequate consultation; hence an Official Publisher's Consultative Committee including representatives of library interests might be appointed to assist the publisher in his task.

Finally, by providing the Supervisor of Documents with an administrative home, the Publisher would supply a base relatively independent of publishing agency pressure, while at the same time furnishing an opportunity for the Supervisor of Documents to communicate with the library community. This the Supervisor could best achieve through membership in the Publisher's Consultative Committee.

Even where centralization of distribution functions is not possible, every province should have an official equipped to provide the editorial services usually offered by a publisher. Such services are badly needed; most provincial government publications are poorly written and unattractive, and they frequently obscure rather than clarify the policy and statistical data they are intended to present. The Official Publisher, or an officer attached to the Supervisor of Documents, could offer such a service. We recommend *that all provinces be urged to appoint an official responsible for improving the quality of provincial publications through the provision of editorial services.*

In describing the duties of the Official Publisher we have not suggested that they include responsibility for central control of the printing function. The omission stems from a need to establish a clear conceptual distinction between the publishing and printing functions. The Publisher is clearly the most suitable official to oversee printing activities. However, where he is charged with this responsibility, care should be exercised to keep it distinct from his role as publisher; he should not be allowed to become a mere buyer of printing, or copying, as most of Canada's provincial Queen's Printers have become.

We have outlined a complex organization whose structure and operation will not be readily apparent. The accompanying charts attempt to overcome this difficulty by describing the relationships between the elements of the Official Publisher and Printer's organization and indicating a probable pattern of work flow.

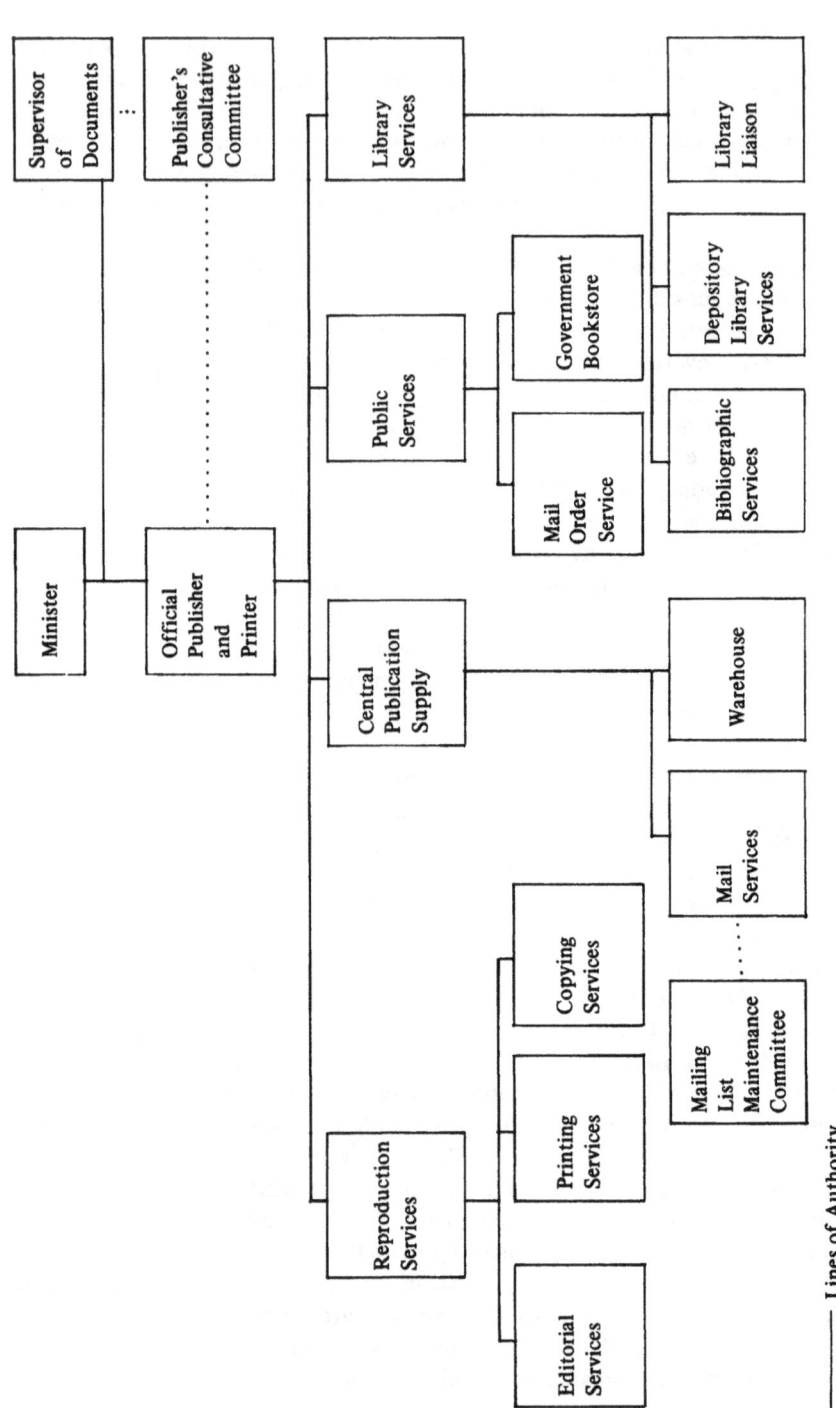

CHART 10:1 A suggested operating structure for an official publisher and printer

Chart 10:1 suggests an operating structure for an Official Publisher and Printer. Although internal services - such as personnel and office supply functions - are not indicated, they could be added without difficulty. Its broad features are uncomplicated. The Official Publisher and Printer and the Supervisor of Documents are each responsible to a minister for their respective functions, and both are advised by the Publisher's Consultative Committee. This committee would meet regularly to review and advise upon the entire range of activities pursued by both officials and would be composed of representatives of publishing departments, governmental and non-governmental librarians, academics, and the general public.

Four divisions would handle the principal activities of the agency. Reproduction services would offer editorial services in readying material for press and would arrange for its printing or copying by government or commercial facilities. Central Publication Supply would store all publications and carry out the physical handling of publications as they are put in the mail. The division would also house and administer government mailing lists, but would have no control over composition of the lists; this would be the responsibility of the Mailing List Maintenance Committee, equipped with a small staff and composed of representatives of the chief mailing departments and of the Publisher's Library Services Division. A Mail-Order Service would be housed in the Public Services Division, since it is relatively easy to transmit book orders to the warehouse and mail-service sections on properly worded requisitions, but more difficult to keep track of payments for publications and to decide what a member of the public wants when he asks for "that green book on household pests." A staff properly trained to work with the public is best equipped to handle such problems and to run the government bookstore. Similarly, members of the Depository Library Service and Library Liaison Sections will know how to serve libraries better than the mailroom and warehouse staff. Establishment of a Library Services Division would provide libraries with a ready and obvious point of contact with the Official Publisher and Printer and so facilitate communication between the two. A Bibliographic Services Section would provide the services described earlier; Depository Library Services would meet the needs of depository libraries, while Library Liaison would look after all other contacts with libraries.

The route followed by a publication from the time it leaves the issuing agency in manuscript form to its arrival in the hands of a user is described in Chart 10:2. Manuscripts would enter the system through the Editorial Services Section and, when readied for press, would be processed through the Printing or Copying Sections. Since the system is designed to ensure that all documents are brought together at the reproduction stage, their classification as internal or public documents is best carried out here. Once their status has been determined, internal documents will be sent to the appropriate agency whilst publications will be sent to the Central Publication Supply Division, which will, in turn, meet

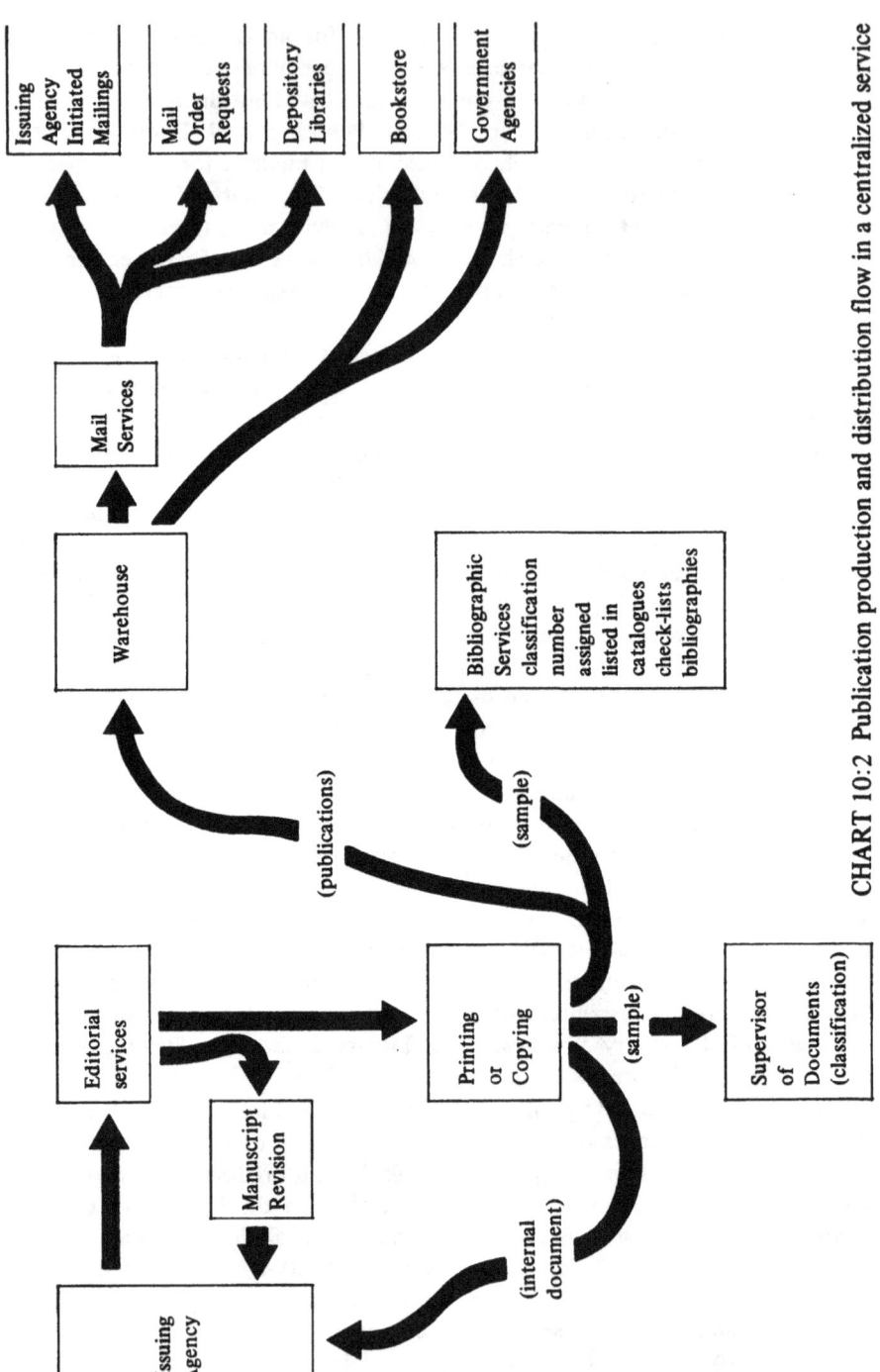

CHART 10:2 Publication production and distribution flow in a centralized service

requests for further distribution from the Depository Library, Library Liaison, and Mail-Order Sections, the Bookstore, and various government agencies. A sample will be sent to Bibliographic Services so that it can be assigned a classification number and entered in various finding aids.

Before concluding our comments on government centralization of production and distribution facilities, some references should be made to the accounting systems used in the provinces. As chapter 3 suggests, there is evidence that some governments, at least, cannot adequately control expenditures on production and distribution. There appear to be many hidden costs in current practices; in some provinces printing contracts are reported to be a major source of patronage; estimates of printing costs are said to be frequently far below eventual costs; uneconomical use of equipment occurs and great waste is sometimes found in distribution as a result of inaccurate appraisals of demand and poor composition of mailing lists. While the data collected in the study is insufficient for authoritative comment, we suggest that *governments would be well advised to review their budgetary and accounting procedures in the publishing field.*

The preceding paragraphs concern the three provinces able to afford centralized distribution systems. In the Prairie and Atlantic provinces the library community must make itself responsible for bringing order out of the current confusion. Therefore, we recommend *that in each of Newfoundland, Prince Edward Island, Nova Scotia, New Brunswick, Manitoba, Saskatchewan, and Alberta, the library community charge (a) specific library (libraries) with responsibility for:* (1) *discovering, locating, and acquiring the publications of that province;* (2) *distributing those publications to depository libraries in Canada and elsewhere;* (3) *providing bibliographic services for its (their) province's publications, including devising a classification formula, reproducing catalogue cards, KWIC indexing, and compiling retrospective bibliographies and cumulative check-lists.*

In other words, the designated library would have to provide the services to libraries that would be provided by the Official Publisher in Quebec, Ontario, and British Columbia. To that end it would have to receive full co-operation from other libraries, including the payment of subscription fees, and it would have to be accorded official status by the government concerned. The designated library need not be a university library, although in many cases only these libraries possess the physical resources needed to provide the service. One or two librarians in public and special libraries vigorously urged that a commercial operation be asked to handle this operation. They felt, very strongly, that the university libraries are ready to demand co-operation from other libraries but do not reciprocate. This criticism may be a valid one; it suggests, at least, that university libraries should review their relations with other libraries. However, it is unlikely that a commercial operation could provide such a service with a profit for itself and reasonable charge to the customer.

Where a university library undertakes to provide such a service, it will be extremely dependent on the legislative library and the Supervisor of Documents for information concerning discovery of documents. In such situations a representative of the university library, the legislative librarian, and the Supervisor of Documents should form a small working committee to ensure the transfer of adequate copies of documents to libraries.

The following comments indicate which libraries, in our opinion, could best provide this service in each of the provinces. Our selection is based on these considerations: (1) a designated library should possess adequate facilities for the task; (2) it should be located in the provincial capital so that it can establish easy contact with administrative offices, and preferably (3) it should have an established provincial documents collection so that the new service can be viewed as a worthwhile addition to existing services.

Newfoundland. The library of Memorial University of Newfoundland possesses the facilities needed to carry out this service, but it would require official recognition as distributor and the assistance of the Legislative Librarian and the Supervisor of Documents in the discovery of documents. *We recommend that the Library of Memorial University of Newfoundland be designated official distributor to libraries of Newfoundland government publications.*

Prince Edward Island. The Legislative Library is the only library capable of carrying out the discovery function. Unfortunately it does not possess sufficient resources for providing bibliographic and distributing services. *We recommend that the Legislative Library carry out the discovery function and that a university library in the Maritime region provide bibliographic and distributing services.*

Nova Scotia. Dalhousie University Library possesses the technical services needed to fulfil this role. However, the discovery function has not been well developed at Dalhousie and close co-operation with the Legislative Librarian would be necessary. *We recommend that Dalhousie University Library be designated official distributor to libraries of Nova Scotian government publications.*

New Brunswick. The New Brunswick Legislative Library has developed a depository system that distributes publications to a limited number of libraries. It is doubtful if this system could be expanded appreciably. Consequently, *we recommend that the Legislative Library be urged to (1) expand its discovery function and (2) continue to receive all publications for deposit in other libraries, but that the University of New Brunswick Library take over all responsibility for distributing publications to other libraries and provide all bibliographic services.*

Manitoba. The excellent service of the Manitoba Legislative Library should not be disrupted. However, *we recommend that the Legislative Library receive sufficient assistance to enable it to expand its coverage of documents provided and to increase the number of libraries served.*

Saskatchewan. At the moment the Legislative Library appears to be the only library capable of providing the service we describe. However, the library and academic communities may have to exert considerable pressure on the government of Saskatchewan to allow the Library to provide such a service. *We recommend that the Legislative Library undertake the distribution of Saskatchewan documents to other libraries.*

Alberta. We recommend that the library of the University of Alberta be designated official distributor, to libraries, of Alberta government publications.

In conclusion, it must be pointed out that none of these libraries could provide such a service without some staff increases. To cover these and other costs involved, a subscription system would have to be introduced.

3. THE ABSENCE OF ADEQUATE PROCEDURES FOR THE DISCOVERY OF DOCUMENTS

In chapter 6 we have presented a number of suggestions that we hope will aid the librarian attempting to discover what documents exist. As we have pointed out, however, few libraries can afford to follow all the procedures we describe. Much time and money would be saved if one or two agencies in each province could perform the discovery function for the general library community. Our recommendations thus far have suggested that appointment of a Supervisor of Documents would ensure that relevant processed documents find their way to the libraries. Similarly, creation of an Official Publisher or designation of certain libraries as distribution agents would also aid considerably.

The provincial legislative libraries could be developed to provide yet another solution to the discovery problem. They occupy a key location within the production and distribution systems, a location which could be exploited to achieve various results highly desirable to the academic and library communities as well as governments themselves.

The means to achieve this end have been suggested and explored in chapter 9 and we shall confine our comments here to a repetition of those suggestions: *Legislative library reference services should be developed to the point where members of a reference research group would be available to assist agency research staff on a continuing basis. Furthermore, all departmental and agency libraries should be integrated in a governmental library system.*

To repeat our earlier remarks, if successfully applied, these measures could achieve optimum utilization of governmental library resources; a better and more extensive flow of information to administrative researchers; a versatile and competent reference staff skilled in providing governments with adequate information in the shortest possible time, and a continuous flow of information concerning government publications to the Canadian library community and thence to the general public and the universities.

It should be remembered that while the provincial legislative libraries ostensibly serve only their own governments and legislatures, they in fact serve a much wider community. In many instances, the services they provide are reciprocated, as, for example, in the case of exchange of publications between provinces. In other instances, however, they receive nothing in return. This is particularly true of the service provided the National Library of Canada, which receives essential information concerning publications that is in turn made available to the general public through *Canadiana*. It has been suggested that as the legislative libraries are here providing a national service, they should be compensated by the national government. Such compensation, if it were applied in some of the directions suggested, would achieve major improvements in information available concerning provincial publication.

4. THE LACK OF AN ADEQUATE DEPOSITORY SYSTEM

Given adequate structures for discovering, locating, and distributing publications, the existing system of depositories should function reasonably satisfactorily. Such structures have been proposed in the preceding recommendations.

There are, however, several factors that are not provided for in existing arrangements. Failure to include limited as well as mass distribution items in depository lists has been a major oversight, and we therefore recommend *that processed as well as printed publications should be considered eligible for deposition in designated libraries.*

Again, only one province, Manitoba, deposits its publications in non-governmental libraries outside the jurisdiction of the provincial government. To remedy this situation we recommend *that certain libraries be designated depositories for the publications of all the provinces.*

In general, we would suggest that only one non-governmental library in each province receive this status, although exceptions would have to be made in the cases of Ontario and Quebec. Smaller university and public libraries should not be encouraged to over-extend themselves in this field. Instead, we recommend *that all universities should be depositories for the publications of their own province, but their collections of other provinces' materials should be highly specialized and geared to specific research interests of the university.*

Not all libraries would wish to receive the full range of even their own province's publications. In particular, they would not possess the facilities to cope with a flood of processed documents. We recommend *that research and general collections be distinguished; the first to receive all the publications of a given government, the second to receive only those documents, or types of documents, it requests.*

Finally, we repeat, libraries must be prepared to pay for depository status. We are not competent to propose how payments might be structured, but suggest that they be created after adequate consultation between libraries and governments.

5. THE LACK OF ADEQUATE LIBRARY PROCEDURES FOR HANDLING DOCUMENTS

The difficulties in acquiring provincial documents have tended to encourage librarians to accord them a low servicing priority. In the estimation of one librarian, Canadian, international, and United States documents are usually acquired and processed before provincial publications for this reason. A given input of work produces a lower output in this area than in any other.[3] The cumulative effect of this tendency has been described in chapter 8. Recommendations suggested to overcome other problems in the provincial documents field will also solve many of the technical problems involved in collection building and resource utilization. In addition, there are a number of further measures that should be adopted by the library community.

A particularly important problem is the question of collection organization and classification. Until librarians agree on classification systems applicable to all the provinces, no progress can be made in the creation of an adequate union catalogue of provincial publications. Because this is a matter of nation-wide concern, we recommend *that the National Library of Canada and the Canadian Library Association establish a committee to determine upon a classification system applicable to all publications of all the provincial governments.*

We suggest, in addition, that an automated system, such as the KWIC system, would overcome many of the problems now associated with applying traditional rules of subject cataloguing to this field. We recommend also *that the National Library improve and develop as soon as possible, its union catalogue of provincial government publications.* Such a catalogue could do much to introduce collection rationalization as would the improvement of interlibrary loan facilities, and we recommend *that the library community explore the possibilities of expanding interlibrary loan facilities in the provincial publications field.*

It will be some years, however, before improvements of this nature can be introduced. There is much that can be done in the meantime. Thus, we recommend *that librarians within provinces and regions discuss and agree upon procedures for rationalizing collections along the lines suggested by our recommendations concerning depository status.* Such rationalization might even include deposition of early legislative library collections in university research libraries, on condition that systems be established that would guarantee the legislative library speedy delivery of requested items. Again, the circulation of duplicate and want lists does not seem to occur as frequently as many would like.

A solution to the problems posed by the scarcity of early publications lies in microfilming documents. An overwhelming majority of libraries questioned on this point declared themselves in favour of such a project. We recommend *that the Canadian Library Association and the Canadian Political Science Association jointly support a project to microfilm provincial government publications.* We suggest that priority be given to microfilming royal commission documents and legislative records (including "newspaper Hansards").[4]

Finally, in order that we may discover the parameters of the field, we recommend *that the Canadian Library Association and the Canadian Political Science Association sponsor projects leading to the compilation of retrospective bibliographies of provincial government publications.*

These recommendations have sought to meet the specific problems enumerated earlier in this study. A few suggestions of a more general nature may be appropriate. In particular, it should be pointed out that the most important recommendation we can make relates not to governments and government libraries, but to "users" and to librarians in general. That recommendation is that *if we wish to see changes made, we must act to bring them about. We must act as a pressure group and we must use the techniques of pressure groups.*

To that end we suggest that the Canadian Library Association and the Canadian Political Science Association, together with other interested groups, establish a continuing joint committee to apply pressure to the governments concerned.

Finally, members of the academic community should remember that no improvements in the current situation can be sustained if we do not maintain a core of dedicated teachers and researchers in the field. There are indications that provincial studies are about to assume the place of importance in Canadian scholarship that they should have occupied long ago. In order to encourage this development, we recommend *that interested political scientists form a subsection of the Canadian Political Science Association that would be dedicated to promoting scholarship in the field.* Such promotion could take the form of sessions on provincial studies at the Association's annual meeting and the encouragement of regional meetings on the subject. The *Canadian Journal of Political Science* could do much to improve the quality of provincial government publications if from time to time it published articles reviewing the publications of given departments or groups of departments.

Provincial government publications do not form a body of great literature. They are seldom satisfactory as a research resource. But they do represent a key to the understanding of provincial government policies and thus of the societies which support them. They are an important part of our historical resource. Yet we have squandered that resource and we are still squandering it. Our wastefulness has made it impossible for government and public alike to achieve adequate understanding of policy issues. The quality of life in Canada has suffered accordingly. By improving the state of official publishing in the Canadian provinces we will not eliminate poverty, abolish pollution, or overcome any of many problems that confront us. But we will have augmented our ability to achieve broad public understanding of these problems and so contributed to their solution.

NOTES

1 / Interview with Mr D. Beeney, Information Director, Ontario Department of Trade and Development.

2 / See chapter 4 for a fuller discussion of the background to this recommendation.

3 / Interview with Mr A.H. MacDonald, the Librarian, Faculty of Law, Dalhousie University.

4 / Interviews produced a variety of suggestions concerning priorities for microfilming. Royal commission documents and legislative records are suggested because they are much used and difficult to obtain. Departmental reports, also frequently suggested, are more readily available.

Summary of recommendations

The following list of recommendations is ordered on a rough priority basis. Rough because it is not possible to pinpoint precisely when each step forward should be taken; some could be put into effect immediately, while others depend on previous action. Ranking was achieved through assessing each recommendation in terms of its attainability under existing conditions, the immediacy of the need it is designed to supply, and its relationship to other recommendations. The resulting list is broken down into three segments: those recommendations attainable in the near future; those attainable within a few years, and those to be achieved only over a long period.

Each cluster of recommendations is preceded by a brief commentary explaining its order; suggesting which interest groups are best equipped to urge each proposal, and indicating which bodies should be approached. It goes without saying that unless there is effective collaboration among all of those interested in gaining these ends, there is little point in presenting them at all.

IMMEDIATE OBJECTIVES

The first group of recommendations demands more intergroup co-operation than government action. By looking initially to these objectives - and some are already half attained - an interdisciplinary group would develop a thorough understanding of the problems involved and would consequently be able to speak with authority when urging other related measures on government. Nearly all these recommendations should be urged by national bodies, such as the Canadian Library Association or the Canadian Political Science Association, but some - such as number 11 - could be left to negotiation between local organizations and government departments. Similarly, the more far-reaching proposals should be supported by as broad a coalition of interested groups as possible. It is also important to find the best place to bring pressure to bear. In most instances the cabinet and the treasury board administrative staff should both be approached.

It is suggested that depository status be sought early in the campaign (and that the attendant rationalization of collections be carried out), since although few libraries will derive much immediate benefit, it should provide them with an incentive to make the designation meaningful.

Recommendation 12 is important because a successful internal review of the situation will make most governments more amenable to advice from interested groups. If an internal review is set in motion, groups should lose no time in presenting all of their objectives to government, since such review studies frequently set the mould for many far-reaching decisions.

The recommendations are:

1. that interested political scientists form a subsection of the Canadian Political Science Association that would be dedicated to promoting scholarship in the field.

2. that the Canadian Library Association and the Canadian Political Science Association jointly support a project to microfilm provincial government publications.

3. that the Canadian Library Association and the Canadian Political Science Association sponsor projects leading to the compilation of retrospective bibliographies of provincial government publications.

4. that the National Library of Canada and the Canadian Library Association establish a committee to determine upon a classification system applicable to all publications of the provincial governments.

5. that the National Library improve and develop as soon as possible, its union catalogue of provincial government publications.

6. that the library community explore the possibilities of expanding interlibrary loan facilities in the provincial publications field.

7. that librarians within the provinces and regions discuss and agree upon procedures for rationalizing collections along the lines suggested by our recommendations concerning depository status.

8. that certain libraries be designated depositories for the publications of all provinces.

9. that all universities should be depositories for the publications of their own province, but their collections of other provinces' materials should be

highly specialized and geared to specific research interests of the university.

10 that research and general collections be distinguished; the first to receive all the publications of a given government, the second to receive only those documents, or types of documents, it requests.

11 that provincial governments be urged to advise recipients when mailing lists are being revised and request them to indicate whether or not they wish to remain on the lists.

12 that provincial governments review their budgetary and accounting procedures in the publishing field.

13 that provincial governments be urged to define a government publication as any document prepared by or for any agency of government and reproduced and circulated to groups and individuals other than those advising or negotiating with the government concerning the subject matter of the document.

14 that all provincial governments be urged to centralize all multi-copying and printing services.

15 that each jurisdiction appoint a responsible official - a Supervisor of Documents - to examine all government documents reproduced in significant quantity and to determine, in conjunction with publishing departments, which documents should circulate only within the government, which should be sent to depository research libraries, which to general depository libraries, and which should receive broad public distribution.

MIDDLE-RANGE OBJECTIVES

This group includes the most important recommendations for reform and will require the broadest possible coalition of interest groups to achieve. It will also require the most persistent pressure at key decision centres such as the cabinet and treasury board staff. In theory, all of these objectives are attainable, although none is, if a sufficient degree of energy and determination is not directed to their achievement.

16 that legislative library reference services should be developed to the point where members of a reference research group would be available to assist agency research staff on a continuing basis.

17   that the governments of Quebec, Ontario, and British Columbia be encouraged to establish or extend policies of centralized distribution.

18   that in these provinces the central distributing agency – the Official Publisher – have responsibility for:
      (a)   operating a government publications bookstore,
      (b)   providing bibliographic services for the province's publications,
      (c)   depositing provincial publications in selected libraries in the province and elsewhere,
      (d)   providing an administrative home for the Supervisor of Documents' office.

19   that in each of Newfoundland, Prince Edward Island, Nova Scotia, New Brunswick, Manitoba, Saskatchewan, and Alberta, the library community charge (a) specific library (libraries) with responsibility for:
      (a)   discovering, locating, and acquiring the publications of that province,
      (b)   distributing those publications to depository libraries in Canada and elsewhere,
      (c)   providing bibliographic services for its (their) province's publications, including devising a classification formula, reproducing catalogue cards, KWIC indexing, and compiling retrospective bibliographies and cumulative check-lists. It is recommended that the following be charged with these responsibilities:
      Newfoundland, the library of Memorial University of Newfoundland,
      Prince Edward Island, the Legislative Library with distribution carried out by a university library in the Maritime region,
      Nova Scotia, the library of Dalhousie University in close cooperation with the Legislative Library,
      New Brunswick, the Legislative Library with distribution carried out by the library of the University of New Brunswick,
      Manitoba, the Legislative Library,
      Saskatchewan, the Legislative Library,
      Alberta, the library of the University of Alberta.

20   that processed as well as printed publications be considered eligible for deposition in designated libraries.

21   that all provincial governments be encouraged to centralize their bulk mailing facilities.

LONG-RANGE OBJECTIVES

These three recommendations either do not demand immediate attention or cannot be attained until the preceding objectives have been achieved.

22   that provincial governments be urged to (1) establish provincial master lists for use in the distribution of publications; (2) provide for adequate administration of the lists through the appointment of an appropriate official.

23   that all provinces be urged to appoint an official responsible for improving the quality of provincial publications through the provision of editorial services.

24   that all departmental and agency libraries should be integrated in a governmental library system.

Appendix I
The questionnaires

In deciding to distribute separate questionnaires to each of the five distinct elements of the investigative field, it was hoped that a specific approach, although complex to administer, would limit the length of individual questionnaires and so improve the rate of return.

This aim appears to have been achieved, but the procedure introduced costs of its own. For example, data relating to several worthwhile collections of comparative materials had to be excluded because we knew that several legislative libraries did not have the resources they would need to answer the comprehensive question on strength of collections that was included in the material sent to university libraries. Assessments of the strength of collections of non-serial publications had to be excluded on similar grounds.

Every potentially significant library collection on the continent was canvassed: questionnaires were sent to the ten legislative libraries, eight provincial archives, forty-seven Canadian university libraries, the Library of Parliament, the National Library of Canada, and thirteen other public or institutional libraries (see Table 1:1). Fifty-five of the eighty responded.

Not all the provincial Queen's Printers completed the questionnaire, but none denied us an interview, and where necessary the questionnaire was filled in at that stage.

Locating distributing agencies within governments proved a difficult task and contributed to the low rate of return for questionnaire 2. The questionnaire was sent to the deputy minister in each department canvassed, in the hope that he would pass it to the key source of information. This stratagem had limited success; many questionnaires were not returned and there was considerable variation in the quality of those that were, even though the response was usually friendly and co-operative.

In general, three departments in each provincial government were canvassed. In order to obtain a degree of standardization, for comparative purposes, and to elicit the views of agencies most likely to have had experience in publishing, the departments of agriculture, trade and industry, and education were selected. This operating assumption proved to be generally correct (we might have approached departments of natural resources and public health and welfare with equal expectations), but the collection of data from these sources might have introduced a bias into the total picture presented in this report, suggesting a more sophisticated operation at the provincial level than may actually exist. We hope that the results of the interview phase of the inquiry offset such a bias.

Similar problems confounded our approach to users of provincial publications. Too numerous to be known or to canvass in their entirety, they had to be selected on a disciplinary basis. Thus, historians, economists, and political scientists were polled, but not geographers, sociologists, or members of professional faculties. The lack of dimension thus incurred was only minimally offset by interviews.

These academics were approached through department chairmen, each chairman being asked to give the questionnaire to interested staff members or graduate students. Despite the obvious drawbacks of this approach, seventy-one individuals responded, and response was sufficiently well distributed in all provinces but Quebec to provide a reasonably accurate assessment of the state of research and instruction in the three fields at most universities. The lack of response from the French-Canadian universities* seriously distorts the degree of academic interest in Quebec affairs, suggesting that this most studied of all provinces has received very little scholarly attention.

*All questionnaires and letters to these centres were composed in the French language.

Questionnaire No. 1: Queen's Printer

AN INQUIRY INTO PROBLEMS RELATED TO THE PRODUCTION AND DISTRIBUTION OF PROVINCIAL GOVERNMENT DOCUMENTS AND THEIR AVAILABILITY TO SCHOLARS

IF YOU WISH TO RESTRICT THE USE OF ANY OF THE INFORMATION GIVEN IN THIS QUESTIONNAIRE PLEASE INDICATE ACCORDINGLY

1. *Duties of the Queen's Printer*
   What are the duties of the Queen's Printer in regard to each type of document referred to? Please check correct column.

Type of document	All work other than writing of document	Calling for tenders from private printing firms and awarding contracts	Printing documents on government machines	Designing layout, typography of documents	Distributing documents to the Public and Government agencies	No responsibility in any of these fields	Other
a) Statutes							
b) Official Gazette							
c) Legislative Papers (bills, order paper, but not debates)							
d) Debates							
e) Journals							
f) Departmental reports							
g) Departmental regulations							
h) Other dept. publications							
i) Reports of boards & commissions							
j) Regulations of bds. & comms.							
k) Royal commission reports							

2   If the Queen's Printer is responsible for the distribution of documents to the public:

    (a) Are distribution lists established:
         (i)   by the Lt. Gov. in Council?
         (ii)   by the Queen's Printer?
         (iii) by the Department concerned?
         (iv)   by the legislature?
         (v)   by any other body?

    (b) Are all published documents automatically deposited in:
         (i)   the provincial legislative library? Yes/No
         (ii)   the libraries of universities in the province? Yes/No (if "yes," please supply a list)
         (iii) the libraries of universities elsewhere? Yes/No (if "yes," please supply a list)
         (iv)   the library of the provincial archives? Yes/No
         (v)   the National Library of Canada? Yes/No
         (vi)   the Library of the Parliament of Canada? Yes/No

    (c) (i)   are provincial government publications advertised to the public in check-lists? Yes/No
         (ii)   are the check-lists Weekly?/Monthly?/Annually?

    (d) Are provincial government publications available:
         (i)   through application to the Queen's Printer? Yes/No
         (ii)   through purchase at a book store operated by the Queen's Printer? Yes/No
         (iii) through retail booksellers? Yes/No

3   Could we please have a copy of the latest annual report of the Queen's Printer?

APPENDIX I: THE QUESTIONNAIRES / 165

Questionnaire No. 2: Government Departments

AN INQUIRY INTO PROBLEMS RELATED TO THE PRODUCTION AND DISTRIBUTION OF PROVINCIAL GOVERNMENT DOCUMENTS AND THEIR AVAILABILITY TO SCHOLARS

Name of Department:
Name of Respondent:/Position

IF YOU WISH TO RESTRICT THE USE OF ANY OF THE INFORMATION GIVEN IN THIS QUESTIONNAIRE PLEASE INDICATE ACCORDINGLY

1   To what extent is your department concerned with the production of the government documents issued by your department?

   (a)   Is your department responsible for all phases of publication (including the awarding of printing contracts)? Yes/No

   (b)   Is your department responsible for all phases of publication (except the awarding of printing contracts)? Yes/No

   (c)   Is your department responsible only for preparing manuscripts for publication? Yes/No

2   To what extent is your department concerned with the distribution of the government documents which bear its imprint?

   (a)   Is your department responsible for all phases of distribution? Yes/No

   (b)   Is distribution handled primarily by another department (e.g., the Queen's Printer)? Yes/No (if "yes," please give the name of that department)

3   If your department is responsible for all phases of distribution:

   (a)   How do you distribute the documents:
         (i)   through a mailing list? Yes/No
         (ii)   through sale at your office? Yes/No
         (iii) in response to written requests from the public? Yes/No
         (iv)   through private booksellers? Yes/No
         (v)   other (please specify)

   (b)   Do you advertise your publications:
         (i)   in newspapers and magazines? Yes/No
         (ii)   in a check-list of departmental publications? Yes/No
         (iii) in the department's annual report? Yes/No
         (iv)   in other ways (please specify)

4   If you use a check-list of departmental publications:

   (a)   How often is the check-list issued? Weekly/monthly/annually

(b) Who receives copies of the check-list:
- (i) officials of the department? Yes/No
- (ii) officials of other government depts? Yes/No
- (iii) members of the legislature? Yes/No
- (iv) the legislative libraries? Yes/No
- (v) university libraries in the province? Yes/No
- (vi) university libraries outside the province? Yes/No
- (vii) individuals who ask to be placed on your mailing list? Yes/No
- (viii) others (please specify)

5 Do you automatically deposit *all* publications in certain libraries? Yes/No (if "yes," please specify)

Do you automatically deposit *some* publications in certain libraries? Yes/No (if "yes," please specify)

(a) which publications are deposited:

(b) which libraries receive them:

6 If available, some indication of the volume of production would be appreciated (e.g., number of copies of annual report, other documents, produced each year).
Have you found that demand for departmental publications has increased in recent years? Yes/No (if "yes," please specify)

7 How large a staff do you have on

(a) production of departmental documents?

(b) distribution of departmental documents?

8 Any further comment you may care to make would be greatly appreciated.

APPENDIX I: THE QUESTIONNAIRES / 167

Questionnaire No. 3: Legislative Libraries and Libraries of Provincial Archives

AN INQUIRY INTO PROBLEMS RELATED TO THE PRODUCTION AND DISTRIBUTION OF PROVINCIAL GOVERNMENT DOCUMENTS AND THEIR AVAILABILITY TO SCHOLARS

Name of Library
Name of Respondent/Position

IF YOU WISH TO RESTRICT THE USE OF ANY OF THE INFORMATION GIVEN IN THIS QUESTIONNAIRE PLEASE INDICATE ACCORDINGLY

I   *Strength of Collection*

1   The following list is believed to be representative of the most important government documents in each province. Would you please rate the strength of your collection by using the following rating scheme: A = strong, nearly a complete run; B = good, more than ¾ of items actually issued; C = fair, ¼ to ½ of volumes actually issued; D = weak, less than ¼ of items actually issued; O = not represented in collection.

Type of document	Rating	type of document	Rating
Legislative assembly:		Lands & Forests	
Debates		Mining	
Journals		Municipal Affairs	
Sessional Papers		Provincial Secretary	
Provincial statutes		Public Health & Welfare	
Departmental annual reports:		Trade & Industry	
Agriculture		*Other:*	
Attorney-General		Royal Commission Reports	
Education			
Highways			
Labour			

2   Please indicate any particular strengths in your collection that have not been elicited in question 1.

II   *Access*

1   Is your library

    (a)   open to all members of the public? Yes/No

    (b)   open to students? Yes/No

    (c)   open to students under special circumstances? Yes/No Please specify:

    (d)   only open to the members of the legislature and civil servants? Yes/No

III *Acquisition Procedure*

1   (a) Is your library a depository for the publications of your provincial government? Yes/No

    (b) If answer to 1(a) is "yes," is your library a full depository or a partial one? Full/Partial

2   (a) If your library is a full depository:
        (i)   do you automatically receive all provincial government publications? Yes/No
        (ii) if "no," how do you go about acquiring those you have not received?
        (iii) if "yes," what procedures do you employ to ensure automatic acquisition?

    (b) If your library is a partial depository:
        (i)   do you automatically receive all provincial government publications to which you are entitled? Yes/No
        (ii) if "no," how do you go about acquiring those you have not received?
        (iii) if "yes," what procedures do you employ to ensure automatic acquisition?

3   If answer to (1) is "no,"
    (i)   how do you learn of the existence of publications?
    (ii) how do you go about acquiring the publications?
    (iii) how would you rate your success in acquiring publications after you have requested them? (i.e., 90 per cent successful, etc.)
    (iv) how would you rate your success in acquiring *all* the publications of your provincial government? (i.e., 80 per cent successful, etc.)

4   If the answer to (1) was "yes," would it be possible for you to send us a copy of the legislation/order in council authorising a depository system?

5   (a) Do you think it would be desirable to have an agency in each provincial government centralize the distribution of all that government's published documents? Yes/No

    (b) If "no," would you give your reasons?

    (c) (i) Has such an agency ever been suggested to your provincial government? Yes/No/Don't know
        (ii) If "yes," what became of the suggestion?

6   (a) Would your library be willing to co-operate with university and legislative libraries in a program of microfilming out-of-print provincial documents held by your library? Yes/No

    (b) Would your library be interested in receiving such microfilms? Yes/No

APPENDIX I: THE QUESTIONNAIRES / 169

IV *Finding Aids*

1   Does your library compile a check-list of your province's publications? Yes/No

2   (a) if "yes," is the check-list issued: weekly?/monthly?/annually?

    (b) to whom is the list distributed?

    (c) how long has it been issued?

    (d) how much staff time is expended in producing the list?

3   (a) Are you aware of the existence of any unpublished bibliographies of provincial government documents? (or of such bibliographies in preparation) Yes/No

    (b) If "yes," please indicate: author, title of bibliography (including period covered), and present location.

    (c) Could it (they) be made available to a qualified person compiling a bibliography for publication? Yes/No (N.B.: This question is asked for information only; it does not imply that such a bibliography is in preparation or even contemplated.)

V   *Addenda*

    Any further comments you might care to make would be greatly appreciated.

Questionnaire No. 4: University Libraries

AN INQUIRY INTO PROBLEMS RELATED TO THE PRODUCTION AND DISTRIBUTION OF PROVINCIAL GOVERNMENT DOCUMENTS AND THEIR AVAILABILITY TO SCHOLARS

Name of University:
Name of Library:
Name of Respondent/Position

IF YOU WISH TO RESTRICT THE USE OF ANY OF THE INFORMATION GIVEN IN THIS QUESTIONNAIRE PLEASE INDICATE ACCORDINGLY

I *Provincial Government Documents Collection*

1 Does your library maintain a collection of provincial government documents? Yes/No

2 If "yes," has the collection:

    (a)   grown gradually? Yes/No

    (b)   been acquired recently? Yes/No

    (c)   been expanded considerably in recent years (e.g., since 1960)? Yes/No

    (d)   been scheduled for expansion in the near future? Yes/No

3 If the answer to 1 is "no," do you intend developing such a collection in the foreseeable future? Yes/No

4 Strength of Collection:

The following diagram attempts to elicit comparative data on the strength of various collections of provincial government documents. It is based on the assumption that the documents referred to (chiefly legislative documents and departmental reports) are the most important provincial government documents. Serials, Royal Commission reports and many other documents have had to be excluded for want of adequate information.

Please use the following ratings:
A = strong - nearly a complete run
B = good - more than ¾ of possible volumes included in collection
C = fair - ¼ to ½ of possible volumes included in collection
D = weak - less than ¼ of possible volumes included in collection
O = not represented in collection

APPENDIX I: THE QUESTIONNAIRES / 171

Type of Document	Province									
	Nfld	PEI	NS	NB	Que	Ont	Man	Sask	Alta	BC
Legislative Assembly:										
Debates										
Journals										
Sessional Papers										
Provincial statutes										
Departmental Annual Reports:										
Agriculture										
Attorney-General										
Education										
Highways										
Labour										
Lands & Forests										
Mining										
Municipal Affairs										
Provincial Secretary										
Public Accounts										
Public Health & Welfare										
Trade & Industry										
Other:										

5   Please indicate any particular strengths in your collection that have not been elicited in question 4:

II *Acquisition Procedure*

1   (a) Is your library a depository for the documents of one or more of the provincial governments? Yes/No

    (b) If "yes," please indicate:
        (i) which provinces have given your library this status:
        (ii) the procedures used to obtain this status:

2   (a) Would you be in favour of declaring certain university libraries across Canada depositories for the published documents of your provincial government? Yes/No

    (b) If "yes," please indicate which university libraries should have this status in your province:

3   (a) Have you acquired the publications of other provinces by direct purchase from the governments concerned? Yes/No

    (b) If "yes," which provincial agencies have been most and least helpful?

	Most helpful			Least helpful		
Province	Name of agency	Fill orders promptly	Standard order procedures	Name of agency	Slow	No standard procedures
Nfld						
PEI						
NS						
NB						
Que						
Ont						
Man						
Sask						
Alta						
BC						

    (c)   If possible, indicate the average rate of success achieved when purchasing directly from governments concerned: 100% successful/50% successful/25% successful

4   (a)   Have you acquired the publications of other provinces by being placed on the free mailing list of various departments? Yes/No

    (b)   If "yes,":
        (i) how was this status achieved?
        (ii) have you had difficulties keeping your library on some of the free lists? Yes/No
        (iii) if "yes," what has been the most common cause of the difficulty?

5   (a)   Do you frequently purchase provincial government documents from book sellers? Yes/No

    (b)   If "yes," do you find
        (i) service satisfactory? Yes/No
        (ii) prices satisfactory? Yes/No

    (c)   If the answer to b(i) is "no," what are the chief problems associated with purchasing documents in this way?

6   (a)   Do you think it would be desirable to have an agency in each provincial government centralize the distribution of all that government's published documents? Yes/No

    (b)   Has such an agency been suggested to your provincial government? Yes/No/Don't know

    (c)   If "yes," please give details.

7   (a)   Would your library be willing to co-operate with university and legislative libraries in a program of microfilming out-of-print provincial documents held by your library? Yes/No

APPENDIX I: THE QUESTIONNAIRES / 173

    (b)   Would your library be interested in receiving such microfilms? Yes/No

III   *Finding Aids*

1   (a)   How does your library discover what documents are currently being published in each province?

Province	Finding aid				
	Check-list from Prov. Leg. Lib.	*Canadiana*	Check-list from Prov. Agencies	Correspondence with agencies	Other
Nfld					
PEI					
NS					
NB					
Que					
Ont					
Man					
Sask					
Alta					
BC					

2   (a)   Are you aware of the existence of any unpublished bibliographies of provincial government documents? Yes/No

    (b)   If "yes," please indicate:

Author	Title of Bib. (including period covered) (Please include bibs. in preparation)	Present location

    (c)   Could it (they) be made available to a qualified person compiling a bibliography for publication? Yes/No (N.B.: This question is for information only; it does not imply that such a bibliography is in preparation or even contemplated.)

IV   *Addenda*

    Any further comments you might care to make would be greatly appreciated.

Questionnaire No. 5: Users

AN INQUIRY INTO PROBLEMS RELATED TO THE PRODUCTION AND DISTRIBUTION OF PROVINCIAL GOVERNMENT DOCUMENTS AND THEIR AVAILABILITY TO SCHOLARS

Name:
University: University status/faculty member/graduate student

IF YOU WISH TO RESTRICT THE USE OF ANY OF THE INFORMATION GIVEN IN THIS QUESTIONNAIRE PLEASE INDICATE ACCORDINGLY

I   Research Activity

1   Are you (have you been) engaged in research involving the use of provincial government documents? Yes/No

2   If "yes," please indicate:

    (a)   the general nature of the research

    (b)   the provinces for which information was required

II   Teaching Activity

1   (a)   Does your department offer (intend to offer) any course(s) dealing wholly or to any significant degree with provincial affairs? Yes/No

    (b)   If "yes," please indicate: name of course, academic level, number of students 1967-8, lecturer, and when first offered.

2   If answer to 1(a) is "yes":

    (a)   Has limited availability of published government documents seriously restricted the scope of the course(s)? Yes/No

    (b)   If "yes," please indicate the nature of the main problems encountered.

III   Finding Aids

1   (a)   Are you aware of the existence of any unpublished bibliographies of provincial government documents? Yes/No

    (b)   If "yes," please indicate: author, title of bibliography (including period covered), and present location.

    (c)   Are you aware of any such bibliographies now in process of preparation? Yes/No

    (d)   If "yes," please indicate: author, address, and title.

(e) Could it (they) be made available to a qualified person compiling a bibliography for publication? Yes/No (N.B.: This question is for information only; it does not imply that such a bibliography is in preparation or even contemplated.)

IV *Availability of Published Provincial Government Documents*

1 Where have you found the bulk of the printed government documents you use?

Source	Material from this source represents what proportion of total? 25% 50% 75% 100%	Collection is excellent good fair poor	Remarks
(a) Your Univ. library			
(b) Another Univ. lib. (please specify)			
(c) Prov. Legislative Library			
(d) Prov. Archives			
(e) Lib. of Govt. Dept. Other (please specify)			
(f) Other (please specify)			
(g) Personal collection			

2 If you have a personal collection of provincial government documents, would you object to stating how you obtained it?

    (a) Through purchase from: Proportion of collection obtained in
        (i) Relevant govt. agency   each way 25% 50% 75% 100%
        (including items distributed free of charge)
        (ii) Bookseller - first-hand:
        (iii) Bookseller - second-hand:

    (b) Through unofficial association with government department

    (c) Through official association with government department

    (d) If you obtained documents by applying personally to provincial government agencies, did you:
        (i) have to apply to more than one possible source? Yes/No
        (ii) have to write more than one letter? Yes/No
        (iii) receive prompt attention to your request? Yes/No

    (e) If you feel the experience gained in acquiring your collection might be of use in suggesting more efficient collection techniques to University libraries, please outline your suggestions.

3 (a) Would you be in favour of declaring certain university libraries across Canada depositories for the published documents of your provincial government? Yes/No

(b) If "yes," please indicate which university libraries should have this status in your province.

V   *Addenda*

Any further comments you might care to make would be greatly appreciated.

Appendix II
Legislative authorization of depository status

Newfoundland
Directive. 21 January 1960. Premier Joseph R. Smallwood to Ministers of all Government Departments concerning Newfoundland Archives.

2. ... it is now requested that you issue instructions to the appropriate officers in your Department to arrange to forward the Archives two copies of all reports, pamphlets, news letters, maps, drawings and other publications *of any kind whatsoever which may be prepared for public issue by your Department from time to time in the future.* ...

Nova Scotia
Management Manual Bulletin 1 OP-31. 17 January 1967.

Two copies of all publications, pamphlets or circulars issued or released by a Department or Agency of the Government for general or limited public distribution shall be deposited with the Legislative Library.

New Brunswick
Order in Council 66-1042. 14 December 1966.

1. Under section 20 of the Queen's Printer Act, the Lieutenant-Governor in Council orders the Queen's Printer to distribute to the Legislative Library of this Province four copies of whatever is published under the Act, but the Queen's Printer may withdraw from the scope of this Order such printing as the Librarian ... exempts.

Quebec
"Quebec National Library Act," 15-16 Eliz. II (1967-8) c. 24.

8. Every publisher of a document published in Quebec shall, within thirty days from the date of publication of such document and at his own expense deliver two copies thereof to the National Library ...

11. Every person who fails to comply with section 8 ... shall be guilty of an offence and liable ... to a fine of $25 to $100 for the first offence and $50 to $200 for each subsequent offence within two years.

Manitoba

Memorandum of an order of the Administrator in Council approved and ordered by His Honor the Administrator on 9 July 1952. No. 1031-52.

Whereas the Legislative Library of Manitoba is a library of deposit of all official publications of the Province of Manitoba for the purpose of assuring preservation of government records and for use by personnel of the government and for reference and research use generally;

Therefore he, the Minister, recommends:

That every department, division or agency of this Government of Manitoba shall deposit three copies of every official publication in any form of printing or processing, available for public information in numbers for general distribution, two of which shall be preserved in the collection of the Legislative Library of Manitoba and one copy to be transmitted by the said Legislative Library to the National Library of Canada.

British Columbia

Order in Council of 25 September 1961.

That the Queen's Printer furnish the Provincial Librarian and Archivist with four copies of all publications printed by him.

www.ingramcontent.com/pod-product-compliance
Lightning Source LLC
Chambersburg PA
CBHW020255030426
42336CB00010B/769